EVERYONE HAS ROOTS

A Star Original

The amateur genealogist has many advantages over the professional. He can develop whatever line of enquiry takes his fancy, he can let his imagination run riot, and he can begin to explore some of the myriad highways an

He will find
like a flash if
ments, that
cannot be pu
a different w
other records
lives of his a
trespassing on their privacy.

EVERYONE HAS ROOTS

An Introduction to Genealogy

Anthony J. Camp

A STAR BOOK

published by
the Paperback Division of
W. H. ALLEN & Co. Ltd

A Star Book
Published in 1978
by the Paperback Division of
W. H. Allen & Co. Ltd
A Howard and Wyndham Company
44 Hill Street, London W1X 8LB

Printed in Great Britain by
Hunt Barnard Printing Ltd,
Aylesbury, Bucks

ISBN 0 352 30195 3

For
Lesley and Owen

Contents

	Foreword	9
1	The Roots phenomenon	13
2	The sources	20
3	The problems	51
4	Migrants	69
5	The possibilities	82
6	Forgery and deception	100
7	The right to Arms	108
8	Surnames and Christian names	130
9	Wider values	145
10	Genealogy as pastime and profession	165

Foreword

This book is a warning. When I was a boy at school I collected the pedigrees of everybody and everything. I ransacked the local library and feverishly explored local histories and memoirs, constructing family trees of anybody and anything from the kings of ancient Egypt to Hitler, from the characters in novels to Lord Beresford's foxhounds. I went through books like the vast *Dictionary of Dates* by Joseph Haydn and extracted everything that might one day be put in a pedigree, covering the floor with enormous tables of the Royal Family written on the backs of National Savings posters.

The pure mechanics of putting these things together, their form and layout, had a particular fascination. That I learned any history from it I rather doubt. It was an obsession which transferred to one's own family may prove fatal. The construction of a family history or genealogy is a never-ending piece of detective work, the number of ancestors doubling in each generation, with limitless possibilities. Anyone who spends any time on it is naturally very pleased with his constructive amateur detection and wants to communicate that joy and his triumphs to others. He rapidly becomes a bore, 'pinning people to the wall', as genealogists say, 'with his grandfather'. The 'fool with a long memory' is avoided by his relations and has no time for family or friends. He will, as a well-known professional genealogist once said, inevitably go either blind or mad! That is the first warning.

One of the pedigrees I thus so lovingly constructed was that of Joseph Stalin. Amongst other books in the public library

I found a life by one of his nephews, Budu Svanidze, entitled *My Uncle Joe*, and carefully added the further details it gave. Over twenty-three years later, with the publication of *The File on the Tsar*, I discovered that Stalin had no such nephew and that Grigory Bessedovsky, when challenged with ghosting the book around someone who did not exist, remarked, 'I write books for idiots'. It is a salutary thought for anyone embarking on the compilation of a family history. That something has appeared in print is evidence of nothing, certainly not of the accuracy of the statements contained therein, and this is particularly true where family history is concerned. The Russians have a saying that a person 'lies like an eye-witness' and it is one that many a genealogist, as we shall see, soon learns all about. Thus he may also become something of a cynic. That is the second warning.

However, some genealogists unfortunately learn nothing of the kind. In their hunger to extend their ancestry just that little bit further or to close that 'gap' which separates them from some well-known family of the same surname they will uncritically accept almost anything that comes their way, however lacking the evidence may be. They are an easy target for the vendors of false arms and Continental orders of doubtful authenticity. They are fairly easily recognisable as the 'social climbers' they so often are, and that may be the third warning.

There is, however, another side to the story. Last year, an actor, when paying his annual subscription at the Society of Genealogists, asked for a receipt for tax purposes. I laughingly enquired if he claimed it as a necessary expense to his way of life and he replied that indeed it was so, the tax man recognising that it was the only thing that kept him sane! When Lord Mountbatten became President of the Society of Genealogists he recalled the difficult years in India and said about the family history he wrote at that time, 'I worked on these books as a relaxation, and in India when I was really kept very busy I found, having finished my ordinary work – sometimes one or two o'clock in the morning – it was a relaxation to spend half an hour in that way, like other people might do crossword puzzles or read detective stories.' Countless numbers of people have found escape in this way and for many a mobile senior citizen with time on his hands it has been a godsend.

Can one claim more for it? The acquisition of a pedigree by a pop star or life peer or the idle curious is only the tip of the genealogical iceberg. The notorious ingenuity of the genealogist, his ability to prove or disprove anything, and his wide knowledge of the exact nature of family relationships and the biographical detail likely to be contained in almost any kind of document has given him a key position in a large number of other studies.

As I shall seek to show from my own experience and from cases which have come to my attention, there is – between the novelist who wants the characters in her latest book put in the form of a pedigree on the end-papers, and the historian who by a minute examination of the land-holdings of the ancestors and relations of Edward IV can discover the financial resources which enabled him to seize the throne – a wide spectrum of uses to which genealogical expertise can be put. At the same time I hope to be able to show something of the sources used and of those who use them, their problems, and what they may hope to achieve.

The idea for this book was that of June Bassett, and if I succeed in it then much will be due to my colleagues at the Society of Genealogists, to Raymond Foster who has worked with me for the last ten years and with whom many of these examples have been discussed, to Alan Rolfe whose patience and ingenuity in the face of these problems has never ceased to amaze me, to Morris Bierbrier for his help with the early descents, to my earlier colleagues at the Society who gave me so much of their time and experience, and in particular to C. D. P. Nicholson and John Phillips, and to those many members of the Society and others whose queries about their searches I have for so long sought to answer.

Chapter 1

The Roots Phenomenon

In 1914 the son of a former President of the United States of America (descendant of a free white emigrant, Matthew Grant, who went from England to Nantasket, Massachusetts, in 1630 in search of opportunities in a new land) had foisted upon him a false pedigree back to the beginning of the sixteenth century and a descent, through another emigrant whose ancestry is not known, from David I, King of Scots.

About ten years ago the son of a professor of agriculture (descendant of a black slave, Kunta Kinte, who was taken forcibly from The Gambia in Africa to Annapolis, Georgia, in 1767, and sold there) had recited to him by the wise men of Juffure his descent from the Kinte Clan of Old Mali through Kairaba Kunta Kinte, a Moslem holy man, who came from Mauretania.

The latter descent, the first of a black American to have been traced through the 'emigrant' ancestor to a specific place of origin in Africa, has been called 'highly questionable' and seems to me to parallel in a remarkably interesting manner thousands of English cases of which the Grant family is only one example. Millions of white American tourists have come to the British Isles in the last hundred years and thousands of black ones are now pouring into Africa. All are hungry for 'roots' and in search of their ancestry. Some whose families have only recently gone abroad will, without much difficulty, discover details of their backgrounds and remaining cousins. Others will be able to do so only after considerable research, perhaps over a long period. Yet others will find it impossible for various reasons to trace anything of their family's origins in the 'home country' and because the need within them to establish some connection is so great they will, without doubt, be easily deceived. The hundred years of searches by the descendants of emigrant families have established this pattern and there is little reason to think that it will ever change.

Alex Haley's moving account of the slave Kunta Kinte in *Roots* (1976), whatever the facts, remains an acceptable generalisation on the appalling fate of thousands of Africans shipped into slavery. Its enormous success in America has been said to derive from its simultaneous appeal to the black American quest for identity and to the white American guilt. I know nothing about the latter, but when Kunta Kinte began to realise that he would never see his home again, 'he could feel something precious and irretrievable dying inside of him forever. But hope remained alive; though he might never see his family again, perhaps some day he might be able to have one of his own.' Many a person in a new environment, cut off from his family and friends, comforts himself, I suspect, with that thought, and it is not only those like the characters in Schedrin's *The Golovyov Family*, who because they have 'no conscious purpose in life instinctively yearn for their native place'. Those families which have left the country for the town and particularly those which have gone abroad, for two or three generations – probably a hundred years – may retain some traditions of their past, but thereafter the memory of what they sprang from will fade. Some insecurity may develop and a need to re-establish some links with the past may become manifest. In any case there may be a natural curiosity as to why the ancestor moved in the first place, perhaps even a lack of sympathy for his assumed motives, and a curiosity as to the fate of those who were left behind, of the cousins mentioned in a few surviving old letters. The discovery of cousins in the country or 'at home' may give some added feeling of continuity with the past and of belonging somewhere, which continual movement, particularly in this century and since the Second World War, has done so much to weaken.

Added to that, many of us have a natural curiosity as to the lives and characters of those who have made us the heirs of so many ages and but for whose existence we should not be here, and in some there is a considerable gratitude for the blessings which have been passed down to them. As Thomas Fuller said in 1662 in *The Worthies of England*, 'I cannot but condemn the carelessness, not to say ingratitude, of those who can give no better account of the place where their fathers and grandfathers were born, than the child unborn. I could almost wish that a moderate fine were imposed on such heirs, whose fathers were born before them, and yet they know not where they were born.' This is not a mere antiquarian interest in the past or escapism but an awareness that we carry in ourselves in a very real sense something of what has gone before. Goethe, when someone proposed a toast to 'Our Memories', knocked on the table and said, 'I do not like these words. The toast seems to imply that we have forgotten something and that some outer event recalls our memories to us. Those things which are great and beautiful never leave us: they become part of ourselves. It is not the past but the eternally new which our desires would have us seek. The new is itself the creation of ever-growing elements of the past. True longing must always be productive and fashion a new and better self.'

Well, for those who *have* partly forgotten there are opportunities now for discovering something of their pasts, opportunities which hardly existed fifty years ago. More people have the means and the time, and increasingly the ordinary person has come to know that there is almost as much to be discovered about *his* background, if he has the time to put into it, as there is about the background of any other person. In the last twenty years a dozen or more popular guides to the subject have been published. The membership of the genealogical societies in this country and abroad has increased enormously in the last few years and thousands of others have with the popular guides mentioned made some attempt to 'climb their family trees'. The attitude to family history as the preserve only of the maiden aunt or the dried-up antiquarian has completely changed, and children in school are encouraged to trace their own family histories as an introduction to other historical studies – though even I become a little worried about teaching history backwards and at duplicated letters from students which begin, 'As part of my assignments in a class in Folklore I am writing the genealogy of my family. I need your help . . .'

When 'Roots' was televised in America it is said that it shattered all American viewing records and that a hundred and thirty million, almost three out of every five of the total population, watched all or part of the series; 'traffic accidents and street crimes dropped dramatically as America stayed at home.' The genealogical societies there were besieged by visitors and inundated with inquiries. One which I received asked plaintively, 'Who am I?', and – perhaps more revealingly – 'and what are my entitlements?'!

Of course, some may envy those who are brought up in a great house knowing all about their ancestors – though often, one discovers, in a most superficial way – knowing that a pedigree was once a sign of noble birth and distinguished ancestry, and thinking that by acquiring a pedigree themselves they may the more easily enter that class. There are others, however, it seems who have an inverted snobbery, and are happy to enter the convict aristocracy of Australia by joining the association of the descendants of those who went out in the First Fleet or to show for good public-relations or political ends that their backgrounds are totally 'working class'.

The curiosity of most, however, is not so prompted. They want to know the truth whatever the facts and they are indefatigable until every detail, however unsavoury, is known. Some will say this when they begin, but when illegitimacy appears or a succession of lowly trades (as for instance that of a street scavenger) is found, they revise their opinions and go silently away to find another hobby. I shall not easily forget the lady who refused to accept that there could ever have been a pawnbroker in her family, and totally rejected all the evidence which proved conclusively that there had been. I have had many similar arguments with persons who cannot accept that the arms which their grandfathers used on their signet rings were unlawfully assumed. Grandfather, who is nearly always a hard-headed businessman and a pillar of respectability, would never have done such a thing!

The other stories which that grandfather cherished may be another reason why people start looking for their ancestors, but when found to be based on the very flimsiest of evidence and distorted out of all truth by succeeding generations they are still the hardest 'traditions' to kill. The speculations of one generation as to their relationships and claims become the certain traditions of the next. Such stories are legion, almost every family has one if not more, and their variety, as showing what people are willing to believe, is quite extraordinary.

A few years ago a magazine in Australia carried a story about one Captain John Boleyn, a descendant of Queen Anne Boleyn (presumably through Elizabeth I!), who married Lady Sarah Percy, daughter of the first Duke of Norfolk (whose surname is Howard), and went to Australia in the 1860s after killing a sailor. 'Our family story was kept very quiet,' the descendant said, 'because the old people were ashamed of the sailor incident.' It is much more likely that such a story was invented to disguise a runaway sailor or a convict, in the same way as stories about emigration to Australia via the Californian Gold Rush have been used to cover convict ancestry. Similarly a family's lowly condition has often been ascribed to grandfather's gambling when, in fact, he was born in the workhouse, was illegitimate, or came from humble parentage.

The number of boys who have run away from Eton, still wearing their school clothes, and gone straight to the colonies must run into thousands! One, I remember, because of his delicate constitution had been taking a special medicine, and the medicine bottle he carried with him was still in the possession of the family! Again, tens of thousands of heiress daughters of ancient houses have run away with grooms or servants, and an equal number of well-born brothers, two or more, went to

America in the early days. (The latter are always invented to explain two unrelated families in the United States at the same time.) All families called White come from the Isle of Wight. All families called Warwick are related to the Earl of Warwick. And Miss West, who reads about the great West Window in York Minster, believes that her family must have come from Yorkshire! If evidence for these events cannot be found, then it has obviously been suppressed. If the parents of a person are shown in a book, then clearly they are only there to put one off the track of the real parents. If they are not shown, then it is because their interests are being protected. The convinced descendant has an answer for everything.

As I have said, it may be the arms used on a signet ring by some long-deceased member of the family, or on a book plate, which will start the descendants off on a search for their ancestry. Again, it may be some story of an abandoned title or of unclaimed moneys. They may have bought some china with a coat of arms on it, or a piece of silver, or moved into a house about which they would like to know the history. They may possess some unusual surname, or the same surname as some famous person of the past or present and be continually asked if they are related.

Whereas it was the fashion in the last century to aspire to a Norman ancestry, as any browser in the old peerages or county histories will soon notice, there is now no particular preference. Following the establishment of the *entente cordiale*, and certainly between the two World Wars, it seems to have been fashionable to invent a French or Huguenot origin for families, if not by ancestral research then by false derivations of names. A surname deriving from an old English place name such as Dennington would be said to come from a de Ninton, and a name like Attick or Atwick, meaning a dweller by a dairy farm, would be said to be French, derived from d'Atique. There has, however, always been a tendency to give unusual English names which cannot be found in the standard dictionaries a foreign origin of some kind. Perhaps middle-class families which could not aspire to county gentry status and

Norman ancestry associated the industry of their forefathers with that of the Huguenots, in the same way as today a family with financial or artistic expertise will often think that it derives from an unknown Jewish ancestor, and set out to discover him. Just prior to the Second World War there were in this country those searching diligently for Jewish ancestry for all sorts of people in order to upset the Aryans! Other families in which some ability begins to show in writing, music, or painting may seek to discover its earlier occurrence in the family, and the descendant of an artist claiming to be a great-nephew of Turner will see publicity and financial advantage when she comes to sell his paintings if the relationship can be proved.

At the same time as there is a growing interest in other things connected with the past – with antiques, local history, heraldry and archaeology, for example – this varied interest in the many aspects of family history has developed. Towards the end of this book I hope to show how people not necessarily interested in family history as such are using genealogical techniques and sources to aid other research. Some of the interests in the subject which I have already mentioned may be of a rather superficial nature, and there is some danger in this because a little amateur dabbling in records can do a very great deal to confirm one's prejudices about the past – those over-simplified views which schooling or upbringing so often accentuate rather than diminish – and so it is perhaps worth saying that those who approach the subject with an open mind, eager to know the truth whatever it may be, and to develop the lives of their ancestors in real depth against the history of their times, will learn not only a very great deal about the past but also about the present.

Chapter 2

The Sources

In the British Isles there is rarely anything to be called instant genealogy. The National Portrait Gallery may advertise 'Take-away History', but the construction of a pedigree takes time, and it may take a great deal of time. There is no sense in rushing in a taxi to that proverbial heaven of the ancestor-hunter, Somerset House, at four o'clock on a Friday afternoon or on the last day of a holiday and expecting to trace a line back to the Conqueror as a birthday present for your father next week, for it cannot be done. Take it slowly in the first stages, perhaps in all stages, but you will perhaps only learn by experience that something done in a rush will almost certainly need doing again. Keep careful notes of what you have done, the periods you have searched, the location and titles of books and manuscripts you have consulted – and the exact wording of what you find there – and keep them in a loose-leaf book from the very beginning, and you will not go far wrong.

I hope that no reader will be put off by the complexity of the records I am about to describe and that those with the time and means available will go ahead and tackle at least some of them. However, because genealogical research takes time and not everyone lives near the records they need, and sometimes because help may be required to read or interpret the documents, you may feel at some stage that professional help would be an advantage.

There are professional genealogists who will undertake the whole of the research work for you or who will give advice on any specific problems you may encounter, and there are record agents who will do specific searches on your instructions. Some of these have a specialised knowledge of particular periods, areas and subjects which would help you over a particularly difficult hurdle, and occasional assistance of this kind need not be expensive. Lists of these professionals may be obtained from the Association of Genealogists and Record Agents, the address of which is given in the last chapter of this book.

The *first rule* in all genealogical work is to work from the known to the unknown, from the present day backwards in time. To take a person of the same surname in the past and to trace all his descendants in the happy thought that you will be one of them is nearly always a complete waste of a considerable amount of time. One of the first things you will almost certainly discover is that your surname is not half as uncommon as you think it is and that 'traditions' of descent from some famous person of the same surname (probably based solely on speculation about the subject two or three generations ago) will exist in some shape or other in practically every family of that name you come across. That is not evidence of relationship to them or to the person involved. There is very rarely anything to be called a 'gap' in a pedigree. A pedigree goes as far as the evidence will take it and then it ends. The further ancestry, when found, is practically bound to lie in the direction least expected. And so perhaps the *second rule* is to approach the matter, as I have already said, with an open mind and not to attempt to force the evidence to meet any preconceptions you may have.

If some work has been done on the family previously – and you may depend upon it that the work which aunt so-and-so did tracing the family back to John of Gaunt has quite unaccountably disappeared – there are very few steps that it is practicable to take before starting the work over again. The files of the great majority of past professional and amateur genealogists no longer exist. The document collection of the Society of Genealogists (at 37, Harrington Gardens, London, SW7) contains some, and others, particularly where arms are involved, may be found at the College of Arms (Queen

Victoria Street, London, EC4). The papers of many of the early antiquaries are in the manuscripts department of the British Library (at Great Russell Street, London, WC1) and others more recent have found their way into county record offices. Those pedigrees of more than three generations in the male line which have been printed in county and family histories, in periodicals and in a host of out of the way and forgotten places, are indexed in two indispensable volumes, *The Genealogist's Guide* by George W. Marshall (1903) and its continuation *A Genealogical Guide* by John B. Whitmore (1953). Although these indexes do not, as Dr Marshall said, take such a low range as to include such works as *The Pedigree of the Devil* by Frederic T. Hall (1883), they are unusually exhaustive. They are being brought up to date in a third volume, compiled by Geoffrey Barrow and just about to be published, listing pedigrees printed since 1950.

These works do not concern themselves to any large extent with Scottish and Irish pedigrees and for these Margaret Stuart's *Scottish Family History* (1930), Joan Ferguson's *Scottish Family Histories held in Scottish Libraries* (1960), and Brian de Breffny's *Bibliography of Irish Family History and Genealogy* (1974), should be consulted. It is as well to remember that references in these which may not seem at all relevant when you commence your searches may become so when your search has progressed a little.

The various lines of ancestry then being researched by members of the Society of Genealogists were listed in the *Register and Directory* last published in 1966 (supplement of new members 1968–71) and the interests of others may be determined from the birth-briefs they file (showing their sixteen great-great-grandparents) the surnames from which are indexed every few years in *The Genealogists' Magazine*. A new venture to index all the manuscript pedigrees remaining in private hands was launched in 1976. This is known as the National Pedigree Index and is administered by a small committee working from the Society of Genealogists. It is suggested that those with pedigrees of more than three generations in their possession should file the details on the printed slips provided by the National Pedigree Index. There is no charge for this, but anyone wishing to have a search made in the Index is charged a fee in advance and asked to provide a stamped and addressed envelope. For this fee, the inquirer is given all the references to one particular surname in the areas he indicates and the addresses of their owners. The fee is refunded if nothing of interest is found.

The Federation of Family History Societies (at 2 Stella Grove, Tollerton, Nottinghamshire) has another index of those persons who collect and are interested in all families of a particular surname wherever they are found – the Register of One Name Societies – and some local Family History Societies have also published indexes to the interests of their members.

The Association of Genealogists and Record Agents (at 123 West End Road, Ruislip, Middlesex), of course, maintains an index of the areas and subjects in which its members are interested from a professional point of view, and some of the members of that Association provide (with the permission of their clients) details of the surnames on which they have worked to the National Pedigree Index.

No index to the pedigrees registered at the College of Arms exists outside the College, but many of the early pedigrees at the British Library are listed in Richard Sims, *An index to the pedigrees and arms contained in the heralds' visitations and other genealogical manuscripts in the British Museum* (1849).

With the high cost of certificates of birth, marriage and death at the General Register Office, and no information being available there except in that form, you will save yourself much expense in the early stages of your search by obtaining as many details as possible from the memories of older members of your family and from any papers, certificates, or family bible entries which may have survived. The date of a birthday inscribed in a book, a note on the back of an old photograph, a probate copy of a will, a treasured war-service medal, some entries in a birthday book, each may reveal something that will make the search easier – or perhaps harder, for remember that entries in family bibles, for instance, are often entered many years after they took place, when the year may well be a guess, and that the memories of the elderly are not always to be relied on where dates and ages are concerned. Remember also that facts apparently forgotten today may well be remembered tomorrow and that conversations with the old are unlikely to reveal very much at one sitting but that much may be discovered over a long period of discussion, particularly round an old photograph album and undeterred by tape recorders. Of course, some people have prodigious memories, and when Mrs Hilda Grenfell came to see me about circularising her relatives in an attempt to raise money for the Talbot House Settlement, which one of them had founded, she reeled off from memory a pedigree of several hundred names without the slightest difficulty.

The basic records of baptisms, marriages and burials in the Church of England have been kept in the various parish churches in this country since the middle of the sixteenth century and have changed very little over the years. Printed forms were introduced in 1754 to record marriages and then, in 1813, baptisms and burials. It was not until 1st July, 1837, that births and deaths came to be recorded as such and the centralised indexes for these and for marriages, covering all England and Wales, were started at the General Register Office in London. They now contain two hundred and forty-five million entries. The office was for years at Somerset House in the Strand but was moved to St Catherine's House, 10 Kingsway, London WC2B 6JP, in January, 1974. Here the quarterly indexes are open to public search, Monday to Friday, 8.30 a.m. to 4.30 p.m. Only the indexes are open to search, the records themselves occupying nine miles of shelving, and no reader's ticket is required or appointment necessary, but equally no information is available except in the form of certificates and each certificate costs £2.50.

The usual procedure is to work from the details on any birth certificate (perhaps your own), searching back from that date for the marriage of the parents, and then, from their ages at marriage, searching for their births, and so on back to the commencement of the records in 1837. Thus it does not help to know that grandfather's tomb is in Wembley churchyard and that he died in 1902 aged 76 and so would have been born in 1825/6, which is before the General Register Office started. You must, if you know the maiden name of his wife, search for his marriage first (as this will give the name of his father), or, if the wife's name is not known, obtain the birth certificate of your father first of all in order to obtain your grandmother's name.

Details of death can be filled in at a later stage, but this may be a difficult task if the names are common, as the death indexes only give ages from 1866 onwards. Death certificates in England and Wales, except since 1968, and unlike those in the United States, in Australia and in Scotland, have never shown the date or place of birth of the deceased, and the parentage is given only for children and some unmarried women. They are, therefore, of little genealogical value. If there are a lot of possible births under the name you are looking for, each one can be checked against the known name of the father for a fee of £1.50 until the correct one is found.

The preparation of a certificate or a check of this kind takes at least twenty-four hours and so several visits to the General Register Office will probably be necessary. The search room is often crowded and searches there may take time and be physically exhausting. It is obviously no place to have a picnic or to take the family, children, or prams, but it is surprising how many are encountered there!

Having taken the family as far as the records at St Catherine's House will go, you will probably end up with a birth in the 1840s or 1850s or a marriage about that time as your first mention of the family. You will probably now be finding it difficult to restrain yourself from going to the place mentioned or from writing to the incumbent of the local church about his parish registers. If you take either of these steps you will, more often than not, be wasting your time. The visible evidences of one's ancestors in any given place are remarkably few and the chance of finding grave-stones in the churchyard about one in ten. There is less than a fifty-fifty chance that the records are still there, and in heavily built up areas the church your first known ancestor married in may well only have been built shortly before your family came there. It may also come as a surprise when you call unheralded at the vicarage that the vicar is rather more concerned with the living than with the dead and that he has no interest whatsoever in your research.

You must be prepared, but in all this you are leaping ahead, for before consulting parish registers there are very few cases in which it is not advantageous to search the Census Returns first of all. A Census has been taken every ten years since 1801, but the first complete set to have survived is that for 1841 and from that date onwards they become available to public search at the Public Record Office, Chancery Lane, London, WC2, as soon as they are more than a hundred years old. In the 1851 Census everyone was asked to give their ages, their relationships to the head of the household, their occupation, and to say where they were born, and similar information appears in the returns for 1861 and 1871. The returns from 1881 onwards remain with the Registrar General at St Catherine's House. In certain circumstances and on payment of a fee of £6 he will make searches in those for 1881, 1891 and 1901 for details of one person at one address, and in some cases of extreme difficulty such a search may be helpful if you can provide the assurances as to the use of the information which the Registrar requires. All the returns are arranged in street order and are produced at the Public Record Office in the form of microfilm. There are indexes of places and often of streets, but not of names, although some local county record offices and city libraries have obtained copies of the returns relating to their areas and in a few cases are making indexes to the names in them.

Using the Census Returns alongside the earliest certificates obtained from the General Register Office, it should be possible to determine the exact dates and places of birth of some members of the family prior to 1837 and perhaps as far back as the 1780s or 1790s, for everyone alive in 1851 in the British Isles (excluding Ireland) must be in the returns somewhere. If the events which the certificates record did not take place near to the date of one of the censuses, then a directory may help to localise the family. Regular annual lists of tradesmen in London have been published since 1740 and they exist for many provincial towns from the late eighteenth century and for all the English counties from about 1830. A complete bibliography of printed directories has been published by the Royal Historical Society showing the libraries where they may be found.

It is from the Civil Registration and the Census that we begin to learn something about human nature. We see how people's ages and places of birth vary in the Census Returns, how they alter their ages when they marry according to the age of their partners; how they register illegitimate children as legitimate; how they increase the social status of their parents when marrying; how, if no marriage certificate can be found, one of the parties is almost certainly married to someone else; and how their ages on death certificates and tombstones are the worst possible indications of their true ages. Of course one must also be on the look-out for cases where the woman has been previously married to a man who has died and has not mentioned that fact when registering the children of her second marriage, thus making a search for that marriage practically impossible, her first husband's name not being known. Moreover, the ages in the 1841 Census Returns are reduced to the next lowest multiple of five, something which Vera Watson evidently did not realise when chiding Queen Victoria in *A Queen at Home* (1952) for her inaccurate return from Buckingham Palace that year on the form headed 'Schedule for Public Institution'!

Having discovered the parish of birth of the earliest known ancestor through the Census Returns, and presuming that the ancestors were thought to be members of the Church of

England, the next step will be to search the Parish Registers of the appropriate church. If it is not clear whether the place mentioned in the Census is a parish, this can be checked in Lewis's *Topographical Dictionary* or Wilson's *Imperial Gazetteer*. A complete list of parish registers for all England and Wales was published in 1831 and forms the basis for the more generally available *Key to the Ancient Parish Registers of England and Wales*, by Arthur M. Burke (1908).

The series of county maps showing parish boundaries published by the Institute of Heraldic and Genealogical Studies at Northgate, Canterbury, Kent is particularly useful for determining the names of other parishes in the neighbourhood.

As I have said, less than half the parish registers of the country remain in the parish churches, the remainder having been deposited in diocesan record offices (generally the same places as the County Record Offices). A list of those deposited in this way has been published by Local Population Studies, *Original Parish Registers in Record Offices and Libraries* (1974, with a supplement in 1976).

The incumbents of parishes were supposed, from 1598 onwards, to send to their bishops copies of the entries in their registers every year. These 'Bishops Transcripts' form a useful substitute if the original registers are difficult of access or lost although they may well not be complete for the years before the Restoration and will always have occasional gaps. Sometimes they give more detailed entries than appear in the registers and both should therefore always be checked. Those for the Diocese of Winchester do not begin until 1770 and those for London until 1800. Again these are generally deposited in the appropriate County Record Office.

However, there still may not be any need to consult the original registers or the bishops' transcripts, for large numbers of both have been transcribed and indexed and a fair number have been printed by parish register societies. Perhaps about a third of the total number of parish registers have been copied in this way. The largest collection is at the Society of Genealogists, which actively organises and encourages this transcription work, and there are others in a great number of local libraries and record offices. Recent catalogues of these have been published by the Society.

The entries in these registers have not generally been collectively indexed in any way but a computer-compiled index now on microfiche to more than twenty-five million baptismal entries for places throughout the British Isles (mainly 1538–1837), which has been made by the Genealogical Society of Utah, is in the possession of the Society of Genealogists. This has a very extensive coverage in some areas and a very poor one in others. A typescript index of about seven million marriages in England only (1538–1837) and again of very uneven coverage, known as Boyd's Marriage Index, is at the Society of Genealogists, and another Index of Marriages, almost complete for the London area but limited to the period 1800–1837 and known as the Pallot Index, is at the Institute of Heraldic and Genealogical Studies at Canterbury. Printed lists of the registers covered by these three indexes have been published.

Everyone has a right to see original parish registers 'at all reasonable times', but under the Parochial Fees Order 1972, fees may be payable to the incumbent of the parish.

The details given in parish registers of the Church of England from their commencement in 1538 to the present day vary to a certain extent from period to period and from area to area. Prior to the introduction of printed forms in 1754 and 1813 the incumbent entered whatever details he wished and some indulged themselves whilst others were sparing and neglectful. However, baptismal entries will normally only give the name of the father and the Christian name of the mother. The marriage entry will give only the names of the couple marrying and, from 1754, the names of two witnesses, and it very rarely includes any details of the parents or of the ages of those married before 1837. The burial entry will more often than not just give the name of the person buried, showing the parentage only if it is a child. The age was not regularly given until the printed forms were introduced in 1813. Dates of birth and death are not generally recorded.

Thus if there are only one or two families of the name in the parish, reasonable identifications of inviduals may be an easy matter, although the register entries themselves give so little detail. It is particularly difficult where a link has to be proved between a person baptised and a person married some twenty or so years later, and this is where other evidence has to be looked for. In such cases the witnesses to the marriage, or a Banns Book, if it has survived, or the details given to the bishop when a marriage licence was applied for, may throw further light on the matter.

The inscriptions in the churchyard may yield additional details of some families, such as exact dates of death, ages, and relationships not revealed by the parish registers. There may be copies of these in the county record office or at the Society of Genealogists. All those in the burial grounds of Hertfordshire, for instance, were copied early in this century and are at the British Library.

Other documents surviving in the parish, but more likely deposited now at the county record office, and varying greatly from place to place, may throw some light on the poorer families. The parochial accounts will not only include the names of those from whom the poor rates were collected, but show how the rate was used in poor relief and in a thousand and one other ways. 'For a sheet to bury Widow King, 4s.' (1628), 'To Abraham Richardson to relieve him in time of lameness and sicknesse and to the chirurgeon to set his bones 15s. 9d.' (1635), 'For a hat for Elizabeth Weller before she was put out to apprentice 2s.' (1645), 'Expenses of carrying John Still's wife and Elizabeth Dymond to London to be healed of the King's Evil 15s. 10d.' (1664), 'For an old coat for Elizabeth Skinner 2s.' (1664), 'For bricks to mend Goody Stace's chimney, 1s.' (1700), 'For drink to the people that helped to set John Waumer's leg 2s.' (1708), are all entries at Cowden, Kent. The continual concern with the poor and the charge which they might become on the parish produces notes about the whipping of vagrants and their being sent away.

From 1697 certificates of their legal places of 'settlement' were required if they were allowed to stay and these provide most valuable indications of movement from one place to another. Later some grant might be made towards their emigration abroad, the latter being a popular method of reducing the population of the workhouse. The fathers of illegitimate children were searched out and charged or made to marry the mothers and pauper children were put to work or placed as apprentices. The original records may survive or a note of the charges in connection therewith may be found in the account books. In some cases these books may commence long before the parish registers. The variety of other documents in the parish chest is wide and may include material on local charities, almshouses, land owned by the church, plans of the churchyard and of pews showing their ownership, diaries and memoranda of former incumbents, and so forth, all well described and explained in W. E. Tate's *The Parish Chest* (1967). It cannot be sufficiently stressed, however, that what survives in one parish may, through neglect, damp, and purposeful destruction, be totally lacking in another.

The records of those from whom the rates were collected – the Rate Books – may themselves be a valuable indication of relative social standing, of length of stay in a parish, of ownership of a particular property, or of the succession of that property from one person to another. Very occasionally, as in any other record of tax collection, absences have to be explained and some such notation as 'died' or 'gone to New England' will appear.

The Church of England has not generally kept registers of its congregations as such, but these are often found with the Nonconformist bodies and may again supply some record of movement from one place to another for members of those denominations. Again they survive very haphazardly, particularly so since of those chapels standing in 1801 only about one in five now remains, and the lack of central organisation has frequently failed to safeguard their records. However, in the last century a great number of the registers of these congregations prior to 1837, together with those of the Chapels Royal, the Foundling Hospital and the Hospitals at Greenwich and Chelsea, were collected at the General Register Office and are now at the Public Record Office. They include about three hundred marriage registers for the period before 1754, recording 'clandestine' marriages at places like the Mayfair Chapel, the Mint in Southwark, and the Fleet and King's Bench Prisons. The Registrar General published a list of these 'non-parochial' registers in 1859 and they relate mainly to the Baptists, Congregationalists, Presbyterians, Wesleyans and Quakers. The Jews and the majority of Roman Catholics would not give up their registers and these generally remain in their hands to this day. Prior to 1837 the registers are mainly of births or baptisms, Lord Hardwicke's Marriage Act in 1754 having made illegal all marriages except those in parish churches and those of the Quakers and Jews, but a few burial registers are found. The detailed registers of the Quakers were copied and indexed by the Society of Friends before being handed over to the Registrar General, and practically all the surviving registers of the Huguenots have been published by the Huguenot Society of London. Similarly, the registers and records of many Roman Catholic congregations have been published by the Catholic Record Society. The extensive centralised register of Nonconformist births kept at Dr Williams's Library in London from 1742 to 1837 is amongst those now at the Public Record Office and so are the registers of the burial ground at Bunhill Fields.

The family relationships tentatively ascertained from parish registers may, if we are lucky, be strengthened and amplified by wills and other probate records. These also, perhaps more than any other documents, may throw light on the personal character of an ancestor, indicate his relationship with other members of his family, and give exact details of his household possessions and of his means of livelihood or the extent and whereabouts of his land. Because regular series of wills exist in some places from the thirteenth century (for example in the Corporation Records of London, Bristol, Exeter, King's Lynn and Norwich) they are the principal and often the only records by which middle-class families can trace any descent prior to the introduction of parish registers. They may indicate family relationships over two, and frequently three and four, generations and bring to light kindred who could not otherwise have been traced, and they have an authority beyond most other records. The number of persons who left wills varied from place to place and from time to time but was something between ten and twenty-five per cent. It was a fashion in some families, and that one has little to leave has fortunately never been a very good reason not to set down something in this way. It often seems the case that those most expected to have left wills did not and those least expected to did! Married women before 1882 could not generally leave wills, but those of widows and spinsters are often particularly detailed. The wills themselves were generally proved in ecclesiastical courts, in the courts of the archdeacons, bishops and archbishops, and there were over three hundred of these, some having jurisdictions in extremely limited areas, but fortunately much has been published about them. The wills are now nearly all deposited in the county record offices most nearly concerned with their areas of jurisdiction. Full details of the courts, their jurisdictions and records, and of the indexes and abstracts which have been published, are given in my book *Wills and Their Whereabouts* which I published in 1974.

The probate jurisdictions of all these courts were abolished in 1858 and since that date a record of all the wills proved and administrations granted in England and Wales is to be found at the Principal Registry of the Family Division at Somerset House, Strand, London WC2. An index is printed annually and gives more detail than the indexes of deaths at the General Register Office.

The indexes of the Estate Duty Office at the Public Record Office provide a valuable centralised guide to the wills proved in the ecclesiastical courts between 1812 and 1858. The wills proved in the Archbishop of Canterbury's Prerogative Court, the best known of the earlier courts, commence in 1383 and are now at the Public Records Office. There are printed indexes of the names of testators from the commencement to 1700, and the Society of Genealogists is presently printing an index to the half-million wills and administrations in the period 1750–1800. Of the local courts, only a few have had their indexes completely printed, Essex being a notable exception (1400–1858).

Inventories filed with probate records are extremely common in some courts' records and may allow the complete reconstruction of a house, its rooms and all its contents. Not all areas are as fortunate as Kent, however, where there are thirty thousand surviving inventories among the records of the Archdeaconry Court of Canterbury. An inventory may throw light on an ancestor's occupation when this cannot be obtained from other documents, for it is unfortunately true that the means of livelihood of many in the past often remains a matter of conjecture even after the most exhaustive searches.

The record of the great majority of apprenticeships unfortunately does not survive and it is only in the period 1710–1810, when the indentures were taxed, that a centralised record was created which is now in the Public Record Office. Before about 1750, the record shows the name of the father of the child apprenticed. They have been copied and indexed by the Society of Genealogists from 1710 to 1774 and indexes of the masters' names have been compiled. Of course, the record of those apprenticed at the cost of a parish, as we have seen, may survive in a parish chest, and those whose apprenticeship in a city company and eventual freedom within a borough gave them the right to practise their trade there were carefully recorded. The apprenticeship records for the Companies of the City of London are chiefly now in the Guildhall Library, Aldermanbury, London EC2, and a centralised index to those achieving freedom of the city throughout much of its more recent history but not open to public search is maintained by the Chamberlain's Court at the Guildhall, London EC2. Similar records survive for other boroughs and, because they generally show the place of residence of the father of the child apprenticed in the town (who may well have married and stayed there), they form one of the chief means by which the origins of city dwellers, particularly those in London, may be traced to the surrounding countryside.

It is not until the nineteenth century, with the advent of the National Schools, that school records exist in any quantity. The lists of scholars at the other public schools have, however, generally been printed and some, like those of Westminster School, have been considerably amplified by their editors. The Society of Genealogists has an extensive collection of these published school registers and with it are the printed lists of scholars at Oxford and Cambridge and at the Irish and Scottish universities. All these generally show the parentage of the scholar and such other details as the editors have been able to obtain. Because it is sometimes difficult to relate the career of a person to his education and early life, the identifications may not always be reliable.

Many of the public school entrants were children of the professional classes, and some details of these may generally also be traced from the published lists of the members of the profession concerned. Printed lists of the officers in the army have been published annually since 1754 but the regular recording of their families did not commence until the nineteenth century with the first general return of officers in 1828. For details of other ranks prior to 1873 the regiment must be known, but if you are armed with that information the Muster Books from 1708 or the Description Books from 1756 or the Soldiers Documents from 1760, all at the Public Record Office, will normally produce the ages and places of birth of all soldiers when they first appear. The records of those soldiers discharged between 1873 and 1882 are in four alphabetical groups, and those between 1883 and 1900 are arranged in alphabetical order in one vast series.

Similarly, the Navy List has been printed since 1749, and basic details of naval officers between 1660 and 1815 may be found in three volumes published by the National Maritime Museum. There are several detailed biographical dictionaries of naval officers, including that by William O'Byrne which includes all the officers serving in 1845. At the Public Record Office the passing certificates of the officers generally have baptismal certificates attached and commence in 1691. For the other ranks, the ships' musters and pay books survive from the end of the seventeenth century, but the ship on which the sailor served must be known before they can be consulted. A list of officers in the merchant service was not published until 1869 and the records of other ranks in that service, which are also at the Public Record Office, do not commence until 1835. The records of those seamen and their dependants who petitioned the Corporation of Trinity House for assistance between 1780 and 1854 are now at the Society of Genealogists.

Copies of the baptismal certificates of the clergy are filed with their ordination papers in diocesan record offices and commence at varying times in the eighteenth century. Many clergy had university educations. Their institutions to benefices are recorded in their bishops' registers and, from 1556, in the Institution Books at the Public Record Office. Crockford's started publishing the *Clerical Directory* in 1858, but there are some earlier printed Clergy Lists.

The annual Law Lists, including both solicitors and barristers, have appeared since 1775. The parentage of barristers may be traced through the records of their admission to the appropriate Inn of Court, three out of four of which have been printed. The articles of clerkship of solicitors, however, which give similar information, do not begin until 1730 and are filed with the records of the courts in which they practised at the Public Record Office. Indexes to them have been compiled.

The records of medical men appear in a variety of scattered sources. The annual Medical Register has been published since 1858, but the unofficial Medical Directory, which gives more biographical information, commenced slightly earlier. Those with medical degrees may be found in the University Lists, but others may be found as members of the Barber-Surgeons Company and of the Society of Apothecaries, or licensed by a bishop. The lives of the Fellows and Licentiates of the Royal College of Physicians have been printed (1518–1925), as have those of the Royal College of Surgeons, but the latter was only founded in 1800.

It is perhaps of interest to consider the possibility of compiling descents from school and professional records alone, and the results are quite remarkable. From the school records it is possible to trace six generations of the Bridgeman family at Harrow, seven generations of the Dolbens at Westminster and eight of the Scotts at Eton, the latter probably a record. Nine generations of the Venn family have been clergy, and all were educated at Oxford or Cambridge. The longest number of successive generations at Oxford University ascertained is ten in the Bagot family, commencing with Walter Bagot of Blithesfield, who entered Merton in 1577, and ending with Lewis Bagot who entered Wadham in 1866. The Aclands had nine generations at Oxford, and six or seven generations there is quite common. Nine generations of the Newcome family have also been clergy, and eight of the Leirs, who were all either Rectors of Charlton Musgrave or Ditcheat in Somerset. Seven generations of the Nicolls family have been in the Army, seven of the Symonds family in the medical profession, seven of the Sandys family in the House of Commons, six generations of the Drake family have sat for one constituency, six of the Gregorys were in the Drapers' Company and six of the Dartons in the Clothworkers'. Five of the Statham family have been in the law, and four generations of the Rumsey family in the medical profession. These are all successive generations.

Biographical dictionaries have been compiled for many other trades and professions. They exist for clockmakers and Members of Parliament, for architects and painters, for sculptors and surveyors, for judges and musicians, and so forth. The names of those in the government departments and the royal household have been published since 1669 in Chamberlayne's *Angliae Notitia* and *The Court and City Register*. I should perhaps also mention the general biographical dictionaries which may be of value for information on prominent individuals, such as the *Dictionary of National Biography* and Frederick Boase's *Modern English Biography*, which is particularly useful for the second half of the last century before *Who's Who* came into being.

For detailed scholarship the thirteen volumes of *The Complete Peerage* are remarkable, giving details of every peer created up to the end of the last century, but for further details of their families and ancestry Burke's *Peerage*, Sir Egerton Bridges's edition of *Collins's Peerage* (1812) and Sir James Balfour Paul's *The Scots Peerage* must be used. All baronets created between the foundation of the order in 1611 and 1800 are detailed in *The Complete Baronetage*, but the knights are less well covered. Most of those created since the Restoration will be found in W. A. Shaw's *Knights of England*. The latter however, only gives the date of creation and the place of residence of the knight.

The mention of printed sources leads one immediately to newspapers and periodicals, a rich but largely untapped source of local and family history. The difficulty is, of course, that very few have been indexed by name and that consequently searches in them take a very long time. Most newspapers published before 1800 are in the British Library and *The Times Tercentenary Handlist of English and Welsh Newspapers* (1920) lists all those which existed prior to that date. Most of the early newspapers in the British Library (at Great Russell Street, London WC1) are in the collection formed by Dr Charles Burney. Commencing in 1619, this collection is extremely valuable for the eighteenth century, all the papers from various sources being bound together in one chronological sequence. The whereabouts of copies of local provincial newspapers between 1700 and 1760 is given in another useful *Hand-List* by G. A. Cranfield. Copies of most newspapers published since 1801 will be found at the British Library Newspaper Library at Colindale Avenue, London NW9.

Entries of births, marriages and deaths in some local newspapers have been indexed, but *Palmer's Index to The Times*, published quarterly since 1791, does not include them. The

Society of Genealogists has a useful index of the deaths reported in *The Times* from 1894 to 1931. A very large number of death and marriage notices appeared in *The Gentleman's Magazine* between 1731 and 1868 and are indexed in the contemporary annual indexes. Separate indexes to the deaths (1731–80) and marriages (1731–1768) have been printed more recently, and many of the deaths, along with those from a great number of other periodicals which appeared prior to 1800 are included in Sir William Musgrave's *Obituary prior to 1800*, published as volumes 44–49 of the Harleian Society series. This includes entries from the *Scots Magazine*, the *European Magazine*, and the *Historical* and *Annual Registers*. *The Gentleman's Magazine* was the sort of periodical found in London's coffee houses in the eighteenth century and the entries therein relate to the class of their frequenters and upwards.

As we have seen, much of the raw material used by genealogists is to be found in County Record Offices. I have mentioned wills and marriage licences, a growing number of parish registers and records, and the bishop's transcripts. All English counties now have record offices administered by the county councils through county archivists. These are freely open to students, usually without formality, although some require an appointment in advance, and it is always safer to give ample warning of one's arrival by post beforehand. They have generally developed from the repositories used by the county authorities for the preservation of their own official records, although they often now contain an immense quantity of material deposited by private individuals. Similar record offices have grown up in large cities for the municipal archives, and others in cathedral towns for the ecclesiastical archives of the diocese. A full list of *Record Repositories in Great Britain* compiled by the Historical Manuscripts Commission (1976) gives their postal addresses, hours of opening, and other details, such as whether or not a guide to the collections has been published. The staffs of these offices cannot be expected to undertake searches themselves, and the genealogist must either come in person, or send a professional record searcher.

Before the Local Government Act of 1888 the Justices of the Peace were the main administrators of the English counties and their records, the Quarter Sessions Records, will form the nucleus of the County Record Office collection. They exist in most counties at least from the mid-seventeenth century, and contain, besides much else, settlement orders for vagrants, bastardy maintenance orders, licences for inns and religious meeting houses, jury panels, sacrament certificates and oaths of allegiance, registers of Papists' estates, lists of travelling salesmen, entries of gamekeepers and certificates for killing game, and the usual indictments, recognisances and petitions, all showing the places of abode and the occupations of those mentioned. Extensive extracts and specialised parts of some have been printed, the complete calendar for Hertfordshire up to 1843 being a remarkable example, and a bibliography appears in F. G. Emmison and Irvine Gray's *County Records* (1961). Here listed are the dates of commencement for each county of the valuable Land Tax Assessments, which may start as early as 1692, and which show the names of landowners, the occupiers, the rateable value and the amount assessed, all this being given annually for each parish in the county. These Assessments took the place of the Hearth Tax, instituted in 1660 and abolished in 1689, which listed all the householders with one or more hearths unless exempted on the grounds of poverty. Generally only the earlier returns survive (1660–74) but they may be useful as giving an indication of the distribution of a surname at that period. In a similar manner the Protestation Oath Rolls of 1641 in the House of Lords Record Office, the Association Oath Rolls of 1696 in the Public Record Office, and the very much later printed *Return of Owners of Land* in 1873–6, may be helpful.

Also with the Quarter Sessions Records in the County Record Offices will be the lists of freeholders, jurors and electors. The names of electors may be more widely available from about 1730 onwards in the form of the printed Poll Books and, after 1832, of Electoral Registers. The Poll Books will indicate the politics of the voter and may indicate family movement, as they invariably show the place of residence of the voter and the place where the land in the right of which he voted was situated. There is a fine collection of Poll Books at the Society of Genealogists and another at the Guildhall Library in the City of London, and catalogues of both have been published.

Other evidence of land ownership in a parish is provided by the Enclosure Awards of Fields and Commons in the eighteenth and nineteenth centuries. The detailed maps which accompany these show most field names and may enable property mentioned in wills to be identified exactly. The schedules attached, like those for Tithe Awards between 1836 and 1860, give the names of the owners and occupiers of the land. The dates for which they survive are included in the accounts of parishes in the *Victoria County Histories* and there are bibliographies of county lists in John West's *Village Records* (1962). Duplicates of the Tithe Awards are to be found in the Public Record Office. The appropriate County Record Office may also have maps relating to turnpikes, to canal and railway developments, of lighting, paving and sewage schemes, as well as other parish and estate maps.

The deposit of estate and family archives by private persons and solicitors anxious to take advantage of the facilities for care, restoration, storage and access provided by the County Record Offices has safeguarded a vast amount of material of potential interest to genealogists. Apart from private letters, household accounts and diaries, there will be quantities of loose deeds, conveyances, leases, mortgages, marriage settlements, manorial surrenders and admissions, and probate copies of wills. If we are lucky, much will have been indexed or calendared by the record office.

Perhaps most important amongst this material will be the manorial records, particularly court rolls, which enroll the changes of tenancy, often by inheritance from father to son, of farms and cottages and quite small pieces of land leased from the lord of the manor. As I have said in *The Genealogist's*

Handbook, 'A series of such inheritances picked out from the court rolls over a number of generations can be as useful as a group of wills to establish a pedigree, and often complementary to wills, which rarely mention houses or land and therefore sometimes make no mention of the eldest son. Like wills, court rolls can be very useful in resolving the ambiguities raised by parish registers when two men with the same names are having children at the same time in the same village, for they cannot both be the tenants of the same farm or cottage.' The court rolls were the effective title-deeds of all copyhold land, but they survive in a very uneven manner. The whereabouts of those for any particular manor may usually be ascertained from the appropriate County Record Office or from the Manorial and Tithe Documents Register, a card index maintained by the Historical Manuscripts Commission at Quality House, Quality Court, Chancery Lane, London WC2.

Although virtually the whole of our county court records prior to 1540 are lost, the records of the national courts and of the centralised administration at the Public Record Office antedate them by several centuries, although after the Reformation there are gaps, especially in the departmental records. Large quantities of records were retained by the Secretaries of State, military governors, and so on, and many are lost to us although others have come into the possession of the British Library and other libraries and some remain in private hands. The Law Courts have always given to those records which have never been out of official custody, the Public Records, a weight as evidence denied to other documents, which are not 'of record' but have to be 'proved' by the testimony of experts.

The oldest Public Records are the rather elaborate charters of the Saxon kings, granting lands and privileges to noblemen and the church and dating from the seventh century. These charters were beginning to be superseded in the tenth century by much simpler sealed writs or letters addressed to the shire courts. They were drafted, copied, sealed and dispatched by the Chancellor, the keeper of the king's seal. From 1199 duplicate copies of these writs or out-letters were enrolled in the Chancery office and they survive in a regular annual series from that date, developing in a very short period into three main series. Firstly, the Charter Rolls recorded grants of land or privileges to churches or cities, or to a man and his heirs. Secondly, the Patent Rolls recorded documents of less importance, such as grants for life, commissions, licences to alienate land, etc., issued in an open manner with the seal pendent. Thirdly, and much the largest series, the Close Rolls recorded documents of a more routine nature issued to local officials in a closed manner which could only be read when the seals were broken. Other series, of less importance, also developed but do not concern us here. The great array of information available on these rolls can only be used by the beginner through the published calendars which exist for the Charter Rolls to 1516 when the series stops, for the Patent Rolls to 1566, and for the Close Rolls to 1500.

The financial administration of the kingdom was extremely complicated, but the main records of the Exchequer, which was heavily departmentalised, are the Pipe Rolls which survive regularly from the reign of Henry II. Extracts from the Chancery Rolls informing the Exchequer of the fines to be collected by the sheriffs were sent to his office in the form of the Originalia Rolls, and the Chancery also made duplicates of the Inquisitions post mortem for the information of the Exchequer. The latter are particularly valuable for the genealogist, recording the inquiry made into the land held at his death by a king's tenant (a tenant in chief), particularising the lands of the deceased, giving the date of his death, and the name, age and relationship of the next heir. These begin in the reign of Henry III and continue to that of Charles II. Some indexes have been printed nationally and others by local societies for particular areas. Similarly the law courts sent Estreats or Extracts of their judgements to the Exchequer, again so that the sheriffs could collect fines, and the accounts of the royal household, the Wardrobe accounts, giving details of royal creditors for instance, were enrolled there.

Among the Exchequer records are the lay-subsidy rolls of the fourteenth and fifteenth centuries giving tax assessments and payments by parish, but not by individual. The returns for the Great Subsidy of 1542–5, however, list all persons over the age of sixteen with an income from land, or with taxable goods with a yearly value of £2 or over, or annual wages of £1 or over. The later subsidies, which continue to the reign of Charles II, are not so detailed but may still be valuable although they show no relationships.

Justice, like the chancery and financial organisation, sprang from the king's household. His itinerant justices steadily reduced the legal competence of the local shire and hundred courts and developed the system of royal writs by which cases were transferred to the central courts, which in due time crystallised out as the two great courts of King's Bench and Common Pleas. The King continued to deal with matters of the highest importance in his own Council, and by the fourteenth century a clear division is seen. The Courts of King's Bench and Common Pleas, fostered by the growth of the Inns of Court composed of laymen comparatively ignorant of Roman law, and the Exchequer which had also developed a Court, dispensed the Common Law, hearing verbal arguments before a jury. The King's Council delegated its authority to the Court of Chancery, founded in the tradition of Roman law, which received only written evidence. The House of Commons championed the Common Law system but with the decline of the Commons under the Tudors other conciliar courts rose in importance – the Star Chamber, Court of Requests, and the Councils of the North and of Wales.

The final separation between the King's Bench and the Common Pleas does not come until the reign of Edward I. The early pleas are classified as Curia Regis Rolls and thereafter they divide as de Banco Rolls (i.e. of the Bench) containing civil pleas between subjects, and Coram Rege Rolls (i.e. before the King) containing criminal actions whether brought by a subject or the crown. They are very poorly calendared. It is, however, in these records that one finds the splendid series of documents called Feet of Fines, recording conveyances of land made as the result of a fictitious action before the justices in order to get the agreement registered between 1190 and 1833.

It is unfortunately true that the difficulties associated with consulting many of the legal records at the Public Record Office are very great. They are huge in bulk, often lack any form of reference other than the name of a county written in the margin of the original and unwieldy roll, and a single case may run through many rolls. Rarely does a verdict appear, so that one does not know if one has found all the relevant proceedings or not. Some of the courts founded in the Tudor period are better served, and the American Bar Foundation has recently published an interesting computer-compiled index to the eight thousand cases in the Court of the Star Chamber in the reign of James I. Much indexing of material in the Chancery and Exchequer Courts has been done by genealogists and an index by the late C. A. Bernau (which is at the Society of Genealogists) contains about four and a half million references to deponents in these courts. Its exact coverage is not completely known, but it certainly contains references to all the litigants in Chancery between 1714 and 1758 and all the county depositions in the Court of the Exchequer taken between 1559 and 1800. The great value of the Chancery records to the genealogist is well illustrated in Robert Garrett's *Chancery and other proceedings* (1965).

With the growth of the office of the King's secretary, the Keeper of the Signet, into two principal secretaries, and then into two Secretaries of State, the great series of State Papers commences, mostly from 1518 onwards. They were the miscellaneous correspondence of officials whose duties knew no fixed limits and they are of the greatest interest. With their growth in importance the Charter Rolls were discontinued in 1537 and the Fine Rolls in 1638. In Henry VIII's reign the Close Rolls also ceased to be used for the enrolment of writs, but the backs of these Rolls continued to be used, as they had been since the middle of the thirteenth century, for the enrolment of private deeds for safe keeping. The State Paper Office was founded in 1578 and the documents were soon divided into two series, the Foreign and Domestic Papers. The two Secretaries of State ran the Northern and Southern Departments, and it was not until 1782 that the Secretary of State for the Northern Department became the head of the newly created Foreign Office. The records relating to Domestic and Colonial affairs have been fully calendared to the reign of George I, but those relating to foreign affairs have not been published beyond Elizabeth I's reign.

The Public Record Office in Chancery Lane was built in 1856 and still houses the great majority of the older of the above-mentioned records, but the new Public Record Office building opened at Kew in 1977 has received all the modern departmental records. Of the classes of records most used by genealogists, the non-parochial registers, the census returns, and the Wills of the Prerogative Court of Canterbury will remain in London, whilst the records of army and navy personnel will go to Kew. The division follows the first two volumes of the great three-volume *Guide to the Contents of the Public Record Office* (1963-8), those records mentioned in the first volume remaining at Chancery Lane and those in volume two going to Kew.

The material in the Public Record Office which may be of interest to genealogists is, thinking in terms of the British Isles, almost entirely limited to England and Wales. However, the Census Returns (1841–1871), include returns from the Isle of Man and the Channel Islands, the Wills include many Irish and Scottish regrants, the Apprenticeship registers (1710–1810) include entries from all the British Isles, and of course the service records contain details of people enlisted in Scotland and Ireland. The great majority of the records for these places however, remain locally.

For the Isle of Man the civil registration of births commenced in 1849, of marriages in 1884, and of deaths in 1877, and the records are with the Registrar General at Douglas. Also at Douglas are copies of all the earlier Parish Registers for the island, and the original wills from 1600.

For the Channel Islands the civil registration began about 1840 and the records are with the Registrar Generals in Guernsey and Jersey. The Parish Registers generally remain in the hands of the clergy. There are wills of personalty in Guernsey (including Alderney) and in Jersey from about 1660, and of realty in Guernsey from 1841, in Jersey from 1851 and in Alderney from 1946.

In Ireland the civil registration of Protestant marriages commenced in 1845 and of all marriages, births and deaths on 1st January 1864, the records being at the General Register Office, Custom House, Dublin. There are separate registers for Northern Ireland from 1st January 1922, at the General Register Office, Oxford House, Chichester Street, Belfast. About two-thirds of the Parish Registers of the Church of Ireland had been deposited at the Public Record Office in Dublin and were totally destroyed there in 1922. These mainly related to the country areas and not to the towns. The present Record Office has made valiant efforts to copy and microfilm the surviving ones. The Catholic Registers rarely commence before 1820 and remain in the parishes, although many have been filmed. The registers of the Presbyterians and Quakers seem better preserved. Because of the absence of registers the churchyard inscriptions have an added importance and many have been copied. Calendars of the destroyed marriage licences have survived for some dioceses and the Irish newspapers are useful for birth, marriage and death announcements. Unfortunately nearly all the Census Returns for Ireland prior to 1901 were destroyed in 1922, as was the bulk of the Irish testamentary records prior to 1904. However, much probate material had been copied prior to the destruction and there are large collections of substitute material at the Record Offices in Dublin and Belfast, and at the Genealogical Office at Dublin Castle. Chief amongst this is the collection of abstracts of all the wills proved in the Prerogative Court of Armagh between 1536 and 1800 made by Sir William Betham. The Registry of Deeds, Henrietta Street, Dublin, contains registered copies of transactions relating to land throughout Ireland since 1708, and these include marriage licences and wills. The registers of scholars at the only ancient Irish university, Trinity College, Dublin, have been printed (1593–1860) and further details of printed and other manuscript sources for the whole of Ireland will be found in Rosemary ffolliott's *Simple Guide to Irish Genealogy*, published by the Irish Genealogical Research Society (7A Duke of York Street, St James's Square, London SW1) in 1966.

In Scotland the civil registration of births, marriages and deaths commenced on 1st January 1855, and the records are at the General Register Office, New Register House, Edinburgh 2, where also are deposited all the old Parochial Registers of the Church of Scotland, some dating from the sixteenth century. In the same building are the Census Returns 1841–1891, all of which are open to public search. At the Scottish Record Office, also in Edinburgh, are the testaments for all the Scottish commissariots from the sixteenth century at least to 1823. Indexes to the great majority of these have been printed to 1800 by the Scottish Record Society. The Registration of Land in Scotland has produced the Old General and Particular Registers of Sasines dating from 1617 in which all land transactions were recorded. Lands held directly from the crown are recorded regularly from 1427 and the general register of Service of Heirs commences in 1600. The Kirk Session Records may, like the records of congregations of Nonconformists or Quakers in England, show movements from one parish to another. The records of the Court of the Lord Lyon, which deals with the registration of arms and pedigrees in Scotland, are at the Old Register House, Edinburgh, and the Scots Ancestry Research Society (at 20 York Place, Edinburgh 1) undertakes research in all the above records. There is a Scottish Genealogy Society (at 21 Howard Place, Edinburgh 3) which publishes a quarterly magazine, and *In Search of Scottish Ancestry*, by Gerald Hamilton-Edwards (1972) provides a background to the whole subject.

All this is rather superficial, as I am only too well aware, and gives no indications of the difficulties and frustrations of research or of the general possibilities, and it is even more difficult to say anything about the records of Englishmen abroad which have been returned to this country without giving a quite false impression as to their completeness. That does not on the whole apply, however, to the records of the British in India, for which there is a quite remarkable collection of material at the India Office Library in London. There are fully indexed copies of the registers of births, marriages and deaths in India from as early as 1698, together with the wills and many copies of inscriptions, and the whole of the records of the personnel of the East India Company.

At the General Register Office, St Catherine's House, London, are the returns of births and marriages (from 1849), and of deaths (from 1859), of British Subjects abroad returned by our Consuls, and returns of births and deaths at sea from 1837 onwards returned by the captains of merchant vessels. Also there are the registers of deaths in the South African and two World Wars, and returns of births, marriages and deaths in the Regimental Registers, 1761–1924, and similar returns from Army Chaplains from 1796 to the present day. A very large number of other miscellaneous returns of British Subjects abroad, dating back to 1627, and fully indexed, has recently been sent to the Public Record Office by the Registrar General and it joins there the other consular returns and registers which form part of the records of the Foreign Office.

At the Guildhall Library, London, is another series of returns from places abroad, this time through the Chaplains licensed by the Bishop of London and generally limited to marriages in the period 1816–1924. Also deposited with the Bishop, and now at the Guildhall, are the registers of British congregations at a number of places from Moscow to Lisbon and from Archangel to the Cape of Good Hope. The inscriptions from the British burial grounds of many such places were copied by indefatigable genealogists like Arthur Leveson-Gower and Colonel Parry at the end of the last century and printed in periodicals like *Notes and Queries* and *Miscellanea*

Genealogica et Heraldica. The problems associated with the movement of persons from and to these places I shall mention later. The records which remain in them remain largely unexplored, but it is clear that they survive quite haphazardly from place to place and what it is possible to trace in one place may be quite impossible in another.

Chapter 3

Problems

In the cold winter of 1592 at Vernham Dean, a little village in the north of Hampshire, Thomas Snell lay dying of the plague. Nicholas Baylye who had lived in that place for twenty-two years, but was a native of Potterne in Wiltshire, 'Hearing of the sickness and infection of Thomas Snell, went to see how the said Thomas did. And they durst come no nearer to the house wherein he lay sick than about the distance of the breadth of an acre and a half. And they then found him lying upon his bed in an open house which they might look through from one end to the other.' He tried to persuade Margaret, Thomas's sister-in-law, 'not to adventure herself so to go to her said sister and brother-in-law, but she answered she would go to them, live or die . . . ' Joan Hopgood, now aged sixty and a widow, of Vernham Dean (where she had lived for thirty-five years), and a native of Henley in Wiltshire, said that Thomas died of the plague and that her own husband, Richard, also died of the plague about ten days after him.

There was a dispute about the will of poor Thomas Snell and the cause was tried in the Consistory Court of Winchester. The depositions from which I have quoted are two perfect examples of the sort of information given by people about themselves in cases of this kind. They show in a most interesting manner the places of origin of two very ordinary people in a way in which no other record would, and such records in the ecclesiastical courts and in the civil courts are legion. They probably contain one of the largest bodies of information about the movements of people within this country, but because of their bulk they remain generally uncalendared and as yet unexplored.

Why, you may ask, are they so important? The simple point is this, that actual records of movement within England are almost totally lacking. There is a popular misconception that 'people did not move about much in those days' but, as Dr Spufford has shown, not only did nearly half the people in seventeenth-century England die in different parishes from those in which they were born, but also a very large proportion of them – including many who died in the parish in which they were born – lived for parts of their lives in yet other parishes. He adds that it was rare for any family to live in one place for more than three generations or a hundred years. Thus any record which shows a family's connection between places has a vital importance to the genealogist.

We can usually trace a family if it stays in the same parish, providing that the normal records have survived and that there are not too many families of the same name in that parish so that identification becomes impossible (and I will discuss this sort of problem later), but once any movement takes place – from one parish to another – then the difficulties start.

There was nothing whatever to stop anyone moving wherever he wished provided he had the means to do so, and in general no one had any interest in recording that movement. It was only for a very few years in the early seventeenth century, for instance, that the series known as Licences to Pass Beyond the Seas was kept – the happy hunting ground of Americans with 'Mayflower ancestry'. These relate to soldiers taking the oath of allegiance before going to serve in the Low Countries between 1613 and 1624. There are some general licences to persons going abroad, chiefly to Holland, for the next eight years, and others to passengers going to New England, Barbados, Maryland, Virginia and other colonies between 1634 and 1639, and in 1677. These have practically all been printed (by Hotten in his *Original Lists of Persons of Quality . . . who went from Great Britain to the American Plantations*, by Jewson in the Norfolk Record Society, vol. 25, and in *The Genealogist*, New Series, vol. 23 *et seq.*) I hope that I shall not offend too many if I say that the 'quality' of the persons and of the lists often leaves a great deal to be desired! This is the sum total of the records of this kind.

However, the increasing burden of the poor, particularly in rural areas from the early seventeenth century onwards, made parish authorities view with great suspicion the arrival of a new man, with or without a family, particularly if it looked as though he would not be able to support himself and would then become a charge on the parish. An Act of 1662 allowed the parish authorities to remove any stranger back to his own parish unless he was able to rent a property to the value of £10 or more. Before making a removal order the Justices making it were required to examine the pauper under oath and to decide what was his parish of 'settlement'. If children were involved, their ages were recorded. The removal could not take place until the persons were actually chargeable to the parish. The charge or costs associated with such a removal would be entered in the account books of the Overseers of the Poor, and if there were any dispute with the parish to which the stranger was returned, as there frequently seems to have been, this would be heard by the local Quarter Sessions and details will be found in the court records. It was laid down in a further Act of 1697 that a receiving parish in which a person wished to settle could demand that he brought with him from his own parish a certificate that he was settled there and that that parish would receive him back again. These 'Settlement Certificates' were carefully kept as the authority for returning a man, and by that chance it has become sometimes easier to trace the movements of a poor family than the movements of the more prosperous classes. Thus a poor man was restricted in his movements, but he could acquire a 'settlement' in a new parish under certain conditions, such as that already mentioned of renting a separate and distinct building of an annual rental of at least £10, or by payment of taxes and dues on property of an annual value of at least £10, or by apprenticeship by indenture, or by hiring for service for a full year to the same man; but if he looked like becoming a charge on the parish, the authorities naturally did all they could to prevent a settlement.

With the settlement certificates may sometimes be found records of the declaration of circumstances of the person involved, which may give many family details. Sometimes these were entered into books and kept in the parishes. Some have been printed. Although the system existed right down into the last century, and was not altogether extinct in this, great numbers of these records have been destroyed. They exist in great quantities in some parishes, and in others there are none at all. They hardly ever seem to have been required from people coming into the City of London, or if they were, practically none have survived. In the London suburbs they exist, uncalendared, in great quantities. Where they have not survived, I have mentioned that some details may be found in the records of the Quarter Sessions if they were disputed, and if the dispute was taken to a higher Court some record may be found in the abstracts by the contemporary, James Burrow, who printed all the cases which came before the Court of King's Bench between 1732 and 1776 in two most fascinating volumes.

The system naturally tended to restrict movement in England generally from 1697 onwards. The problem of tracing the origins of the people who moved into London before and after that date illustrate some of the sources available.

The population of London in 1600 is estimated to have been about two hundred thousand. At some time in the middle of the century London overtook Paris and Naples, to become the largest city in Europe. In the 1690s the contemporary statistician Gregory King estimated the population of the City as about 530,000, and modern demographers think that he was right and that by 1700 it was 575,000. London, therefore, nearly trebled in size in the course of that century, and this despite the plagues which struck the city from time to time. In 1603 over 33,000 people died in the plague, in 1625 over 41,000, and in 1665 nearly 69,000, besides 29,000 who died from other causes. As the death rate was in any case higher than the birth-rate, there must have been an enormous excess of immigrants into London over emigrants from it. As the total population of England was then about five million, this must have been the most significant population movement in seventeenth-century England.

This growth in the size of London affected many parts of the country. By 1640, as Dr Peter Spufford has pointed out, the corn growers of Cambridgeshire, south-east Essex and north-east Kent, the dairy farmers of Suffolk, the graziers of the south midlands, all looked to the London market as the hub of their economic universe. Beyond this, London exerted an enormous influence all along the east coast of England, importing vast quantities of malt from Norfolk, butter from Lincolnshire and Yorkshire (through Boston and Whitby) and, of course, increasingly large quantities of coal from Tyneside and Wearside. Although much research has been done on the sources of the food and fuel consumed in London, little work has been done on the origin of the Londoners themselves, mainly because of the lack of sources readily available. But where there is trade, then there is population movement also.

From the figures I have mentioned it would appear that throughout the seventeenth century about 8,000 more people came to London every year than left it. John Graunt, writing in 1662, said of the Plagues of 1603 and 1625 that in two years, 'The City hath been repeopled, let the mortality do what it will.' The Stuarts in this period had been the first to experiment with estate development, but it was the Hanoverians who raised estate development to the level of an art form. The city they bequeathed to the Victorians was the wonder and envy of the whole world. However, as far as the working classes were concerned, the shortcomings of London's housing, health and Poor Law administration revealed in the 1830s' Commissions of Enquiry suggest that all the eighteenth-century advances were pitifully inadequate. Agricultural labourers, vagrants and Irish immigrants were pouring into the City, often encouraged by the relative generosity of the Poor Law administration in London, which in turn was a burden to the middle-class parishioners. The established residents of west London no doubt wanted to wipe out the districts in the east and drive their inhabitants back to the countryside from whence most of them had come. To them the economic contribution made to London by the migrant slum-dwellers – and there were vast seasonal migrations of labour – was far from apparent. In the nineteenth century London expanded and inflated like a balloon suddenly filled with gas. The area covered trebled between 1800 and 1860 to 121 square miles, and the population rose from 860,000 to nearly three million.

The exact place of origin of the most recent immigrants into London in the nineteenth century can, fortunately, if their exact places of residence in the metropolis are known (and it is surprising how often people moved about within limited areas in London) be discovered from the Census Returns taken every ten years from 1851 onwards, as I have described elsewhere. It is before the nineteenth century that the difficulties start.

One source of information is the registration of wills of Londoners in the various London courts, and in particular in the Consistory Court of London and in the Prerogative Court of Canterbury. Dr Spufford examined the first hundred wills proved in the former Court in its register for 1679–82. Of these, some thirteen gave clues to an origin outside London. These clues are of three kinds – legacies to the poor of provincial parishes, legacies to named relatives in the provinces, and legacies of land situated in the provinces. Ann Purslow, widow, not only left forty shillings to the poor of the parish of Farndon in the County of Northampton, but added 'where I was borne'. The will of Mary Beale, widow, is less explicit. She left money to the poor of Steeple Bumpstead in Essex, but it seems likely that she was born there. John Sharpe, citizen and leather-seller, left twenty shillings to the bell ringers at Wymondham in Norfolk, and it would thus be surprising if he did not have some close connection with that place. At a later period I have found a packer in London, Matthew Brown, mentioning his brother Robert in Warwickshire in 1758, and a property-developer in Kensington, Stroud Lincoln, in 1849 earnestly requested his relations to keep in order the grave of his father and mother in the parish churchyard at Beccles in Suffolk. These wills show movement over a vast area, but only a small proportion of wills give this kind of information. If one in ten left wills, as seems to have been the case, and one in ten of such wills give such useful indications, then the origins of only one migrant in a hundred will be discovered in this way. The proportion of will-leavers in London, however, may be a good deal less than this.

At least in the seventeenth century the frequency with which migrants to London came from a considerable distance, however, was in distinct contrast to the normal pattern of population movement in seventeenth-century England, which was over relatively short distances. Dr Buckatzsch, working on the records of the Cutlers Company in Sheffield, has shown that nearly two-thirds of the migrants into Sheffield in the second quarter of the seventeenth century who became cutlery workers came from less than twenty miles away. In the last quarter of the century only one-ninth of the migrants came from further than twenty miles. Of course, these are still quite considerable distances to search over if the direction from which the migrant came is not known.

It is perhaps worth emphasing again here that marriage entries in English parish registers do not show the names of the parents until 1837, and even then it is only the name of the father which appears. Thus a man marrying in London in 1760 may, if we are lucky, say that he was from such and such a place, or the Banns called may give this information, or the Licence, but the entry, more likely than not, will say nothing of the kind, will not give his parentage or his age, and his place of origin will have to be determined from other sources. I mention marriage licences and I should perhaps add that it was only for a short period in the 1820s that the archbishops required a baptismal certificate to be filed before a licence for marriage was issued.

The chance reference in a will is rather like a chance reference on a tombstone, but the burial places of people who lived in London are by no means easy to find. The burial grounds of most churches in the City have long since disappeared and been built over, all having been closed in 1852, but the inscriptions from all those surviving have been printed by Percy Rushen in *The Churchyard Inscriptions of the City of London* (1910). The inscriptions in the churches themselves have been copied in four volumes at the Guildhall Library by Arthur John Jewers. Together they represent a very small minority of the people buried. The great cemeteries in the outskirts of London which proliferated from the 1840s have excellent individual records, but it is still a major problem to discover where any particular body was taken to be buried. If you can discover a stone you may be lucky and find, for instance, that John Plowes, buried at St Paul's in 1812, was of Leeds, Yorkshire, or that Joseph Steele, buried at All Hallows Barking in 1835, was late of Acrewalls, Cumberland, or even that Abraham Sutton, to whom there is an inscription in the churchyard of St Andrew Undershaft in 1675 was a 'Merchant, lived in Flanders in Ghent, about 30 years and died there 24 May, 1675, in his 55th year'. In more recent times a newspaper obituary may well say something about the earlier life and place of origin of the deceased.

The trouble is of course that these sorts of records, wills, marriages by licence, monumental inscriptions, and so on, will on the whole relate to the families which possessed property of some kind or another, and there are often other ways in which people of that class can be traced. In London and Middlesex there was a registration of the buying and selling of land, and of long leases, from the reign of Queen Anne onwards. This is unique in England, the only other county having such a registration, until modern times, being Yorkshire. A person coming to London and buying property there might well appear in this Registry and this may show where he came from. The development of the great estates in London in the eighteenth century, however, and the use of short leases makes many such people untraceable in these records, which are now at the Greater London Record Office, Middlesex Records.

In England the right to vote was based on a property qualification, for generations a 40s. freehold, and the lists of those voting in London show where their property lay. This might be a useful indication of movement, as when Charles Remnant of Wooburn, Buckinghamshire, votes in London in 1802 because of property he owned in Little Essex Street in the Strand, but it is often more useful in tracing movements within the country than into London. This is due to a large extent to the fact that the members of City Companies in the City of London had the right to vote as 'freemen of the City'. If a man was a freeman, however, your problems are generally solved, for it is this class of person whose place of origin is most easily traced. Until the end of the eighteenth century you could not practise a trade within the city boundaries unless you were a freeman of the City. There were three ways in which you could get such freedom, namely, by patrimony, by servitude or by redemption. To become a freeman by patrimony you had to be the son of a freeman who was such at the time of your birth. Obtaining your freedom by servitude meant serving an apprenticeship in one of the so-called livery companies. On completion of such apprenticeship you were admitted a freeman of the company and this qualified you for the freedom of the City. Obtaining your freedom by redemption meant being admitted by paying a sum of money for the privilege (generally £2. 6s. 8d. in the seventeenth and eighteenth centuries), but in this case you were not a member of a livery company and had none of the privileges attached to it.

From the end of the seventeenth century, however, membership of a Company did not necessarily mean that you practised the trade of the Company, you joined it for the honour and privilege and might be earning your living in quite a different way. Be that as it may, the registers of apprentices of these Companies, some of which survive from the fifteenth century, are a particularly valuable source of information about the place of residence of the father. Most of them are now deposited at the Guildhall Library in the City of London, and several have been printed. For instance the Paviours' Company

Apprentices show in 1670 the apprenticeship of Richard, son of Richard Rogers of 'St Tallbons' in Hertfordshire to Thomas Goodwyn, and in 1712 those of the Cutlers' Company show that James son of James Ragg of Little Leake in Nottinghamshire, 'gardiner', was apprenticed to Thomas Cox. What is true of City Company apprentices in London is also true of borough apprentices in the great provincial cities, in Bristol, Exeter, Norwich, and so forth.

Outside these City Companies apprenticeships were not usually registered anywhere, the indenture drawn up being purely a private deed arranged between the parties concerned. Between 1710 and 1810 however, as we have seen, there was a tax on these indentures, and a central record resulted. They normally show the name and place of residence of the parent up to about 1760, and these are one of the greatest indications of movement throughout the British Isles in that period, being of course particularly valuable for tracing people coming into London to be apprenticed. The records from 1775 to 1810 remain unindexed, but they do not show the places of origin in the way in which the earlier ones do.

Through the apprenticeship records of the city companies it is sometimes possible to trace a descent in London for several generations – perhaps as many as eight or nine – and then to trace the family out of London to their place of origin in the country. Outside the City, however, London families may with the aid of the Census Returns be traced to the end of the eighteenth century, but before that it is usually impossible to know who the immigrant was and one may well search for a baptism in London when that person was born in the country and vice versa. The appearance of families of the same surname in London in an earlier period is rarely any guide, as most English surnames are found in London from the seventeenth century onwards.

These few records which indicate movement may be supplemented of course by others which show movement for particular classes or professions. The regular granting of yearly licences by the Quarter Sessions to a highgler or badger or other travelling salesman, as also to those who had gun licences, may well indicate a move from one parish to another within the same county. Other regular lists of this kind, particularly those where a tax or rate is being collected and non-payment has to be explained, may indicate absences and give the reasons, not only when a man has *migravit ab hac luce* ('migrated from this light,)' as the depositions in the ecclestiastical courts say, but when he has migrated to some other more earthly place.

I have mentioned apprentices as an indication of movement and school and public school records do much the same, although it is often difficult to associate the child educated in one place with the later person whose career has been discovered in another. Clergy, of course, had to provide baptismal certificates when they were ordained, and so did Naval Lieutenants when they took their examinations. The movement of a dancing master from London to Bath, as the late C. D. P. Nicholson once demonstrated to me, may be traced by his advertisements in the local press, and so on. It is the expertise of the genealogist which is tried most of all by problems of this kind, when the later history of a person and of his children may have to be developed in order to obtain some clue as to an earlier place of origin. The places of marriage of children in one generation, for instance, may indicate visits to aunts or uncles of an earlier generation.

Where there has been a change of occupation as well as a change of residence, then identification may become impossible and it is not often that one finds such a useful commencement to a will as that in 1842 of Frederick Benson, 'formerly of Kings Mews, Charing Cross, optician, and since of Hercules Buildings, Lambeth; Montfort Place, Kennington; and Ordnance Terrace, Chatham, but now of 8 Lower Sloane Street, Chelsea, superannuated Clerk of the Admiralty Office, Somerset House'.

I said at the commencement of this chapter that if a family did not move it could normally be traced unless there were so many of the name in the parish as to make identification impossible – and that is an important proviso. Many names in this country which one has not encountered during one's life and which are therefore thought to be 'uncommon' are quite deceptive. They may be uncommon in general but very high concentrations of them may well exist in particular areas, sometimes for no very obvious reasons. The clan system in Scotland resulted in great numbers of families with the same surname. In Lancashire few seem to have migrated from the area and high concentrations of local surnames result, but all over the country there are parishes where strange surnames are relatively frequent, like the Culpeys in Elizabethan Fulbourn, or the Beechenos at Elsworth, or the Shillings at Swavesey, all in Cambridgeshire, and the identifications become difficult.

In London, at Bow Creek, a long thin peninsula almost enclosed by the Thames and known locally as Bog Island, there were out of a total of 160 on the school roll in 1929 at least a hundred children called Lammin, and most of the rest were Scanlan or Jeffries.

Thus even in the last century, with the Census Returns to help us, it is often impossible to trace families with common surnames back to the commencement of Civil Registration in 1837 unless there remains some family knowledge which takes the pedigree back to the 1870s. When Ralph Atherton was searching for the birth of a George Atherton who was known to have been the brother of his ancestor, Frederick, he found 114 George Athertons in the indexes between 1844 and 1875. At Bitton in Gloucestershire there are 138 entries relating to the surname Brain in twenty years in the eighteenth-century parish registers. When searching for the baptism of Samuel Lord, who was known to have been born at Newchurch about 1809 from his age in the 1851 Census Returns, we found eight possible entries in the registers there, of whom only two or three could be eliminated by early burial and other sources. A search for the possible death dates of some met with thirty possible entries in the first five years at the General Register Office.

There is no easy answer to problems of this kind. The expenditure of much money on certificates at the General Register Office may solve some problems after 1837, but before that date one can only build up pedigrees of all the families of the name in the village, using every possible source, in the hope that some conclusions, even if only tentative, can be reached.

There has always been some resentment against the taking of Census Returns. When the idea was first suggested it was called 'totally subversive to the last remains of English liberty' in the House of Commons, and there are always those, often with something to hide, who take pleasure in giving incorrect information here and to the Registrars of Births, Deaths and Marriages. I hope that they realise the difficulties they are giving to future generations! John Lennon's grandfather, a freight clerk in Liverpool, said in the only Census Return in which he can be found that he was born in the place, but if that is so his birth does not seem to have been registered. That is possible, as there was no penalty for non-registration until 1874. Perhaps the hand-written indexes of births at the General Register Office are faulty and the entry has been missed in the indexing. That is also quite possible. We believe that almost ten per cent of the wills proved in some courts have been missed from the contemporary manuscript calendars, and there is no reason to think that the early indexes of births are any better. No search has been made for his baptism in Liverpool as that would be a lengthy task, complicated by the fact that his age as given at death does not correspond with that which he gave in the Census. It may well, in fact, be that he was born in Ireland, but if a birth was found at about the right time there, how would one prove that it was the same man in view of the statement in the Census? Such difficulties are only too common and may completely thwart the construction of a pedigree before it has hardly begun.

Where some mistake is made in an entry in a Parish Register it is just possible that it may be corrected in the Bishop's Transcripts, but if one says that a child is called Matthew and the other that she was Martha (as with one of my Camps at Cottered in Hertfordshire in 1759), nothing will resolve that, or at least nothing that I have yet found has resolved it, for in genealogy hope springs eternal. At neighbouring Shephall, the burial in 1767 of one *Benjamin* Parker 'aged as is asserted 90 years' did not seem to fit into the pedigree of the Parkers at all until I found in the Poor Book that year, 'Paide for buring *Joseph* Parker the charge of £1. 4s.' He had been in the receipt of parish relief at the rate of 1s. 6d. a week for at least eight years.

Ringo Starr's grandfather was John George Parkin, a boiler maker in Toxteth Park, Liverpool, and the son of George Henry Parkin, who worked in the shipyard. George Henry died when his son was only six years old and his widow Mary Elizabeth married Richard Henry Starkey, a driller. The little boy took his step-father's name, as do many others in the same circumstances, but when marrying found himself in difficulties. Giving his name as John Alfred Parkin Starkey, he said that his father was Henry Parkin Starkey. Thus if it had not been for the family's remembrance of the real facts it would have been impossible to trace the pedigree further. Judging by other cases of this kind one might have assumed that he was illegitimate and looked for his birth registration in the name Parkin, and in this case might thus have stumbled on the correct entry only to reject it. Many illegitimate children, not knowing how to show their fathers' names at the time of their marriage, often invent a father's name which is the same as their own or give the name of their mother's father instead, and this obviously causes problems for the genealogist.

The problems of tracing the parentage of illegitimate children, however, are nearly always great. Entries like that in the account book of the overseers of the poor at Stevenage in 1730, 'Charges expended on Joseph Newton and his getting Widow Moss with child and then marrying her £4. 6s. 6d.', are unfortunately not all that common, though a good number of maintenance orders, like that against 'Sarah Catlin of Kimpton, spinster, and Henry Wingrove of Stevenage, baker, for their son William', 1822, do appear in Quarter Sessions Records, and should certainly always be searched for.

I have been interested to find a long descent entirely in the illegitimate line, but the most I have found is four generations stemming from the illegitimate Sir Gerard O'Lally, an Irish Jacobite in the French service, through his illegitimate son Thomas Arthur who was executed at Paris in 1766, and the latter's illegitimate son Trophime who came back to England and had a daughter, Elisa, by Elizabeth Halkett, niece of Lord Loughborough, prior to their marriage. I do not doubt that this rather curious record could be bettered!

The difficulties of tracing the parentage of illegitimate children have been surpassed in this century by those associated with the tracing of the parentage of adopted children. Prior to the Adoption of Children Act, 1926, the adoption of a child of parents of good social standing was governed by the terms of a deed drawn up by the parties involved and no change of name took place. When in 1798 Mrs Fitzherbert adopted Minnie, the youngest child of Lord Hugh Seymour, because he was actively pursuing a naval career and his consumptive wife was off to Madeira for her health, no thought of appointing her the child's guardian entered their heads. But in the space of three years both were dead and a long and bitter dispute ensued in the Court of Chancery, their executors seeking to appoint another guardian. The argument that the child was of a delicate constitution and 'knew no other mother than her', as Mrs Fitzherbert said, has been heard often since then, but as usual availed nothing. It was only after the case had gone to the House of Lords and following the intervention of the Prince of Wales that the head of the family allowed her to keep the child. It is of some interest that in a document attached to her will, Mrs Fitzherbert referred to Minnie and to an adopted niece as 'my two dear children', giving one good cause not always to take such things at their face value.

During the course of the nineteenth century the barbarity with which the unmarried mother and her child were treated abated a little. 'Children begotten in sin would naturally inherit their parents' weakness' and would 'contaminate the minds and morals of the lawfully begotten'. This had been the reason advanced against their being admitted to any institution or orphanage, but with the foundation of Dr Barnardo's Homes and the Waifs and Strays Society, institutions were provided to take in and care for such children. They began to alleviate the situation created by the practice of baby farming – for the desperate situation in which unmarried mothers had found themselves had encouraged them to place their babies with families willing to take a child, often as a business venture. The view that adopting families only wanted the children in order to exploit them was slow to die, but increasingly adoption gained widespread acceptance as a cloak for illegitimacy, as when Frances Stevenson officially adopted Jennifer, the daughter she had had by Lloyd George. It was helped considerably by the emotional appeal of children who had lost their parents in the First World War. As the authors of *The Other Side of Adoption* (1977) say, 'These war orphans in need of homes made a great impact upon the national conscience and hundreds of hitherto reluctant people came forward with offers of adoption'.

Those people who had protested at the inhumane treatment of illegitimate children saw adoption as a means whereby the truth about the child's real origins could be concealed and through this he could be made acceptable to the rest of the community. In 1925 the Tomlin Committee reported that the Adoption Agencies acted in 'the belief that if the eyes can be closed to the facts, the facts themselves will cease to exist so that it will be an advantage to an illegitimate child who has been adopted if in fact his origin cannot be traced.' Thus the Adoption Act of 1926 deliberately sought to fix a gulf between the child's past and future, and provided that the records at the General Register Office which made the connection between the adopted name and the original name of the child should be kept secret, access only being gained with special permission from the courts. The surname taken was always that of the adoptive parents, the Christian names were very often changed, and a new birth certificate provided in those names. The numbers adopted rose to about twenty thousand a year by the mid–1940s, of whom four out of five were illegitimate.

The feelings of many of these children as they grew up seem to me to express in an extreme form the reasons why people so often want to trace their ancestries. Of course, many accepted the situation and asked no questions, but others 'could not ignore the questions that formed again and again in their minds:– Who am I? Where did I really come from? Where are my roots? Why is it wrong to ask? These questions had to do with deep feelings about their own personal identity. They did not want a contrived identity which was based on deception and pretence. They wanted the truth – whatever it was.' Because of it they were accused of ingratitude towards their adoptive parents and many were made to feel guilt about their desire to know. Some went to extreme lengths to discover their real parentage, as *The Search for Anna Fisher*, by Florence Fisher (1975) revealed. One young man who had unusual Christian names which seemed to have nothing to do with his adoptive parents went patiently day after day through the indexes of births at the General Register Office page by page, looking for those names until he found the correct entry.

After much lobbying the law was changed and since 1975 adopted children over the age of eighteen in England and Wales can see their original birth registration after having been interviewed by an experienced social worker called a Counsellor. There is no complementary right for the mother to find out what happened to her child and to be told its adoptive name. Of course, a mother who thought that she had seen the last of her child and whose family was quite unaware of its existence might view with mixed feelings its sudden reappearance, and when, in 1976, the matter received some publicity, headlines like 'Haunted by the Past' and 'Mums in Fear of Knock at the Door' appeared in the *Daily Mirror* and *News of the World*. In some cases there has been intense joy in being reunited, but other contacts have resulted in bitterness and suspicion. There are some very moving examples of those who have embarked on such a search in *The Other Side of Adoption*, with much practical advice as to how to go about it, but in spite of all the problems one can only conclude with its editors that 'knowing is infinitely preferable to not knowing'.

Chapter 4

Migrants

The records of those coming into this country from abroad have certain problems associated with them but there are often other compensations, mainly resulting from rarity of name and the limited sizes of their congregations, which may make the tracing of a pedigree back to the immigrant a much easier task.

From earliest times there had been settlements of Jews in this country but they were totally expelled by Edward I in 1290, although a medieval Jewish ancestry has been claimed for the Isaac family of Patrixbourne in Kent. It seems likely that Jewish families called Inglis and Inglesi in Spain and Gozzo descend from these English exiles. Jews were not allowed to settle in England again until 1655 in the time of Oliver Cromwell, although there were a few in London in Elizabethan times and the pedigree of one, a purveyor of groceries to the Queen, was recorded by the heralds. By 1680 there were about two thousand of them in London, mainly Iberian or Sephardic Jews descended from the refugees of Spanish oppression in the fifteenth century, who came to England via Portugal and other parts of the Continent, particularly the Low Countries.

They were always a closely knit community and were on the whole wealthy, invariably leaving wills, and their synagogue records being particularly detailed and well kept, they are on the whole easily traced. Most difficulties associated with the tracing of these families come from the fluidity of their surnames, as they very often used a different surname for the purposes of trade. Thus Abraham Israel de Sequeira of Bury Street, London, traded there under the name of Gomez Rodriguez. Some, perhaps to obtain social or political advancement, had their children brought up as Christians, and one such, the ancestor of the Barons Eardley of Spalding, changed his name from Gideon to Eardley.

In contrast to the Sephardic Jews the Ashkenazim were often poor refugees from oppression in Russia, Poland and Rumania. They came later than the Sephardic, some from Germany in the eighteenth and early nineteenth centuries, but most after 1880 fleeing from eastern Europe. Many arrived in England penniless and settled in the East End of London because the Anglo-Jewish community there went out of its way to welcome them, setting up in Whitechapel a Board of Guardians to look after their welfare. In this area of London they found synagogues in Stepney and opportunities for keeping their dietary laws. Many were tailors, cabinet makers, cigar makers, old clothes dealers or pedlars, but a minority, like the Goldsmids and Rothschilds, had considerable wealth.

Jews of both varieties have tended to translate or Anglicise their original names, particularly on conversion to Christianity, and although there are two or three hundred such changes recorded in Phillimore and Fry's *Index to Changes of Name, 1760–1901*, the overwhelming majority were changed without formality. Francis Palgrave, the historian father of Francis Turner Palgrave, the editor of the *Golden Treasury*, was the son of a stockbroker called Meyer Cohen and assumed his mother-in-law's maiden name at the time of his marriage in 1823. Lord Swaythling's ancestor changed his name from Montague Samuel to Samuel Montagu. Towards the end of the seventeenth century Mordecai, son of Moses, came from Hamburg and bought a house in Magpie Alley off Fenchurch Street in London, where he was known as Mordecai Hamburger. Becoming prosperous, he chose to be known among gentiles as Marcus Moses, whilst his eldest son was Moses ben Mordecai when among Jews, but Moses Marcus to the outer world. A family thus founded appears to stand equal chances of being known to later generations as Moses, Moss, Mordecai, Marcus, Marks, Hambro or Hamburger.

Certain adoptive names became favourites – Davis, Henry, Ellis, Lawrence and Morris, whilst the Hebrew Zevi, meaning a stag, might first be translated into German as Hirsch or Hirschel, and then anglicised into Hart or Harris.

England has long had a reputation for giving sanctuary to people escaping oppression, recognising that their skills have often added much to our prosperity, whilst sympathy sometimes tempered the resentment which might be felt at their competition and the very fact that they were 'foreigners'. It was for a long time English policy to invite Flemish weavers to settle here but there were several local risings against them. They came to London, York, Winchester, Bristol, Abingdon and Norwich; Frenchmen came to the ironworks on the Sussex weald; and Germans came as armourers to London; and in the sixteenth and seventeenth centuries the variety of immigrants and their trades was considerable. An increasing number were Protestant refugees and in 1571 a quarter of the whole population of Norwich was of foreign origin.

There were two main waves of French Protestant or Huguenot refugees, the first beginning about 1550 and the second mainly following the Revocation of the Edict of Nantes in 1685. These set up their own churches in England and for several generations continued to use their native tongue. Many settled in London, mainly in the area around Spitalfields and here there are still a few of their houses to be seen with their extra wide top-floor windows which were designed to allow maximum light for the silk-weaving looms. Others settled further outside London, at Wandsworth, or in the provincial centres of Norwich, Canterbury, Southampton, Bristol, Exeter and Plymouth. Thirty volumes of their registers have been published by the flourishing Huguenot Society of London, although practically all their churches have now disappeared, their congregations rapidly declining in the early nineteenth century. Their records are particularly full, but the difficulties associated with the tracing of their families arise from the changes in the spelling of their names. These are often anglicised, so that Batteleurs becomes Butler and Pertuis becomes Pertwee, or translated, so that Le Blanc becomes White and De La Rue appears as Street.

The majority of the early French-speaking refugees came from the Low Countries and not from France; other Frenchmen came via the Low Countries, Switzerland or one of the German states, adding further problems to the tracing of their exact place of origin. Many of those who came here passed on, of course, to Ireland, where there was a large settlement at Portarlington, and to America, adding a further dimension of difficulty to the tracing of the pedigrees of their descendants in those countries.

We must not forget the poor people from the Palatinate who came through Holland and England in 1709 seeking a new life in the New World, many of whom stayed in England, and the large numbers of people of German origin who came to England as a result of the close connection which existed between Hanover and England from 1714 to 1837, and which brought in many people connected with the Court. Sir Anthony Wagner, the present Garter King at Arms, in his *English Genealogy*, for instance, recalls that his first ancestor here was Melchior Wagner, the son of a hatter to the ducal court at Coburg who became hatter to George I. Sir William Herschel, the astronomer, first came to England as an oboist in the band of the Hanoverian Guards in 1755.

In the second half of the eighteenth century great numbers of Dutch traders (the great majority of whom, however, did not reside in England) invested in the English public funds, and because of this their wills received a second probate and were copied into the records of the Prerogative Court of Canterbury, an interesting example of the aid which might be given to genealogists abroad by records in this country.

The older registers of the French, Dutch, German and Swiss Churches in London are all deposited at the Public Record Office.

Those who came to England to escape the terror of the

French Revolution in 1789 mostly returned to France later. The poorer among them may be traced to some extent if they stayed, through the grants in aid given to the French *émigrés* in England which are recorded in the Bouillon Papers in the Public Record Office, the Prince de Bouillon having been appointed the administrator of the funds given to these refugees by the British Government. They were Catholic and the difficulties in tracing them are the same as those associated with any other Catholic family in this country, those of locating irregularly kept registers maintained in secrecy, often by itinerant priests, here made worse by the difficulty of identifying grossly anglicised names in Protestant marriage registers.

There were smaller influxes after the second and third French revolutions, and there were other refugees from European countries following that year of revolution, 1848. Other notable groups included large numbers of Russians who came to London after the Russian Revolution, and of Poles after the Second World War. Many of those coming in this century have changed their names and their ancestries may in the years to come be difficult to trace because of that, and because of the relatively poor quality of our civil registration records.

'Foreigners' of another kind, who came south with the Stuarts, and then following the 1715 and 1745 uprisings, and then again in the early part of George III's reign when the Earl of Bute was Prime Minister, are the Scots, but the origins of these, like those of poor Irish and other travellers over very long distances prior to the Census Returns, may often be quite impossible to trace. Their surnames and the Christian names they used may give some clue as to their ultimate origins, but if one is fortunate enough to find, for instance, in that scurrilous magazine *The North Briton*, in the lists of those who voted in London in 1769, 'John Murray, a Scot, alehouse-keeper, Savoy', and 'John Hume, Pall-mall, shoemaker to the King, a Scot', who is to say whether it was they or their parents who came to London, and from what part of Scotland did they come?

The chief means by which real foreigners coming into

England can be traced are the acts of naturalisation and the returns of aliens which have been printed for 1509 to 1800 by the Huguenot Society. These cover all the acts in that period, not just those relating to Huguenots. These indexes are continued to the present day at the Public Record Office, but the records themselves may only be consulted after they have become a hundred years old. They nearly always show the exact place of origin of the immigrant in the country from which he came. The page to George III, for instance, Christopher Papendick, was described as 'formerly of Hanover, now of New Windsor, gent.' at his naturalisation in 1795. Henry Kolle, a London merchant whose grandson changed his name to Horton, was naturalised in 1802 as 'Henrich Kolle son of John Kolle by Sophia Kolle his wife, born at Verden in the Hanoverian Dominions in Germany'. It must be remembered, however, that a large proportion of the foreigners who came into this country, particularly after the Napoleonic Wars, never sought naturalisation but by their marrying English women and producing children born in these islands, their families automatically acquired English nationality. Fortunately the later Census Returns tell us exactly where these people came from, and if one Census does not give that information then the next may do so.

The situation with regard to those moving away from this country is much worse, particularly, as Harold Lancour has said, when you consider that 'the ravages of fire and time have left to succeeding generations but little of the all too incomplete documents made by the shipping and port authorities in those early days'. It is thus unfortunately true that unless some exact indication can be obtained from the records in the receiving country of the emigrant's place of origin in the British Isles, the chances of picking him up here may be very remote indeed. If the emigrant married and had children in this country before emigrating, the chances are greater as there are more records to be found, but if his only appearance in British records is a baptismal entry in one of twelve thousand possible parish registers, many of which will not survive from the period in question, then the difficulties are obvious. One may search for a possible mention in a father's or in some other relation's will, by extracting all those of the appropriate name in this country, but unless the surname is uncommon that is an extremely daunting and wearisome task, and the results may well still be very inconclusive if not worthless.

Even when after much research a tentative identification can be made, it is often quite impossible to prove a positive relationship. An Edward Camp was baptised at Hunsdon in Hertfordshire in 1634 and disappears from the parish. Another Edward Camp who was born about that time turns up in New Haven, Connecticut, and is the progenitor of a vast family in America, but who is to say that it is the same man and that the child at Hunsdon did not die young and his burial go unrecorded as so many infant burials did? Of course, if he had gone in the nineteenth century and married or had a child here after 1837, then that record could be found at the General Register Office and one's problems are solved, but where Scotland is involved that would not be true until 1855, and in Ireland until 1864.

Just as no one in England much cared about who moved from one place to another if he was able to support himself, so they cared even less to record the movement of persons who left the country altogether, and even when they did begin to do so, which was not until 1819, the records kept were fairly inadequate. When E. M. Jones looked at those for South Africa, when studying the group of settlers who went there in 1820, he found on the passenger lists persons who had failed to embark but whose names remained on the list; the names of others who, having embarked, disembarked at subsequent ports of call such as Gravesend or Plymouth; and then, from other sources, a clear indication that yet others had taken their places without being entered on the lists at all. If that happened in the nineteenth century, then almost anything could have happened two centuries before.

This regular series of passenger lists of persons leaving the United Kingdom by sea did not commence until 1819. Lists of passengers ere given to the officers of the port of exit by the masters of the ships involved and were then forwarded to the Board of Trade for statistical purposes. Late in the last century the Board of Trade destroyed all those dating from before 1890, but those from 1890 onwards are at the Public Record Office. They are arranged by year, under the port of departure.

Very fortunately copies of these lists were generally deposited in the port of entry in the country of destination and they survive there. It was from those in the Public Archives at Cape Town that H. E. Hockly was able to form the basic lists for his *The Story of the British Settlers of 1820 in South Africa* (2nd ed., 1957). They were studied in greater depth in E. M. Jones, *Roll of the British Settlers in South Africa: Part I: up to 1826* (2nd ed., 1971). These lists do not in general show even the county of origin in this country, let alone the exact parish, but in the case of the South African lists one can get some idea of the areas involved from the places of origin of the persons who organised the various groups.

This is not, of course, so with the vast numbers who entered American ports. The records there from 1819, with a few others from 1798, are now in the National Archives at Washington. They survive for ports on the Atlantic Ocean and the Gulf of Mexico and for a few inland ports. None survive for ports on the Pacific coast, or for people coming by land from Mexico or Canada. San Francisco was established as a port of entry in 1849 but all the records up to 1936 have been destroyed by fire, either in 1851 or in 1940.

Unless the port of entry, the name of the vessel or the approximate date of arrival is known a search in these American lists is often a protracted task. Those of persons entering Australian ports have to a large extent been indexed and are available at the Mitchell Library. Those in Canada, in the Public Archives in Ottawa, do not go back further than 1865 although there are a few earlier lists relating to subsidised British emigration schemes.

I am often asked if records of their passengers were maintained by the great shipping companies, but that seems most unlikely ever to have been the case. There is certainly no suggestion of it in *Shipping: a survey of historical records* edited by Peter Mathias and A. W. H. Pearsall (1971).

Prior to 1820 the situation with regard to lists of persons leaving this country is chaotic, and lists, when found, like the later ones do not often show exact places of origin here. They may thus not be very helpful from the genealogical point of view, although they may at least indicate the nature of the household that emigrated, the number of persons involved and their relationships, so that one knows exactly what events of marriage and baptism of children one may find in this country, and naturally if the origins of one passenger are known this may itself lead to the origins of others who came from the same area. As Sir Anthony Wagner said in *English Genealogy:*

> We know that in 1632 the ship *Lyon* sailed from London to Boston, Massachusetts, and that several of the families on board came from particular parishes in Essex, and settled in Roxbury and Cambridge, Massachusetts. Knowing this the first place where we shall look for the origins of other passengers on the *Lyon* will be in these and neighbouring Essex parishes. In the same way we know that between the 1830s and 1850s many cutlers from Sheffield settled at Bridgeport, Connecticut. Sheffield is accordingly the first place we shall search for the origin of any unidentified cutler who appears at Bridgeport in those years.

The problems of tracing the origins of emigrants in this country when no actual record of their place of origin exists are extreme and very little appreciated. Sir Anthony, in his chapter on 'Settlers' describes the whole background to American emigration but I can only indicate some of the varied sources from which much has been printed and those that remain to be explored. Where the United States are concerned, what has been printed is calendared and described in great detail in that indispensable book *A bibliography of ship passenger lists 1583-1825; being a guide to published lists of early immigrants to North America*, compiled by Harold Lancour (New York

Public Library, n.d.). The unexplored sources remaining in the Public Record Office in London are described in the article by R. F. Monger, 'Emigrants in Public Records' in *The Genealogists Magazine* (xvi, 135-143, Dec. 1969).

Much of the material on convict transportation there has been explored in such works as L. L. Robson, *The convict settlers of Australia* (1965) and M. and J. Kaminkow, *Emigrants in bondage* (1967), and Peter Coldham is now publishing other convict material from Quarter Session and Assize records. The general background of this subject is well described in A. G. L. Shaw, *Convicts and the Colonies* (1966), and the nature of the records, where Australia is concerned, in John Cobley, *The crimes of the first fleet convicts* (1970). The convicts are well recorded. It is the free emigrants who are difficult to trace.

The extensive use of newspapers made by agents canvassing for emigrants in Northern Ireland and the other sources there, both for free and compulsory emigration, are described in R. J. Dickson, *Ulster Emigration to Colonial America* 1718–1775 (1966). The use of land grants and this book to trace the places of origin of the Irish in South Carolina is described in detail in Jean Stephenson, *Scotch-Irish Migration to South Carolina 1772* (1971).

Shaw in *Convicts and the Colonies* has some interesting figures about the small number of persons transported from Scotland, and for emigrants from that country one should consult the bibliography to Donald Whyte, *A Dictionary of Scottish emigrants to the U.S.A.* (1972). Papers relating to emigration schemes for the Highlanders are in the Old Register House at Edinburgh and no doubt papers of similar sorts of schemes exist in this country and have not been explored. A perfect example is the papers of Dr Barnardo's Distributing Homes which had sent 18,000 destitute children to Canada or Australia by the time of his death, and another is the older Female Middle Class Emigration Society founded by Maria Rye in 1862. The papers of the latter Society and of its various successors down to the Women's Migration and Overseas Appointments

Society, are now in the Fawcett Library. They were extensively used in Una Monk's very interesting little work *New Horizons; a hundred years of women's migration* (1963).

Earlier schemes to encourage the emigration of poor persons who might become a charge on the Poor Rates of English parishes are known, the cost of the passage being paid by the parish. Michael Burchall, working on vestry minute books and overseers' accounts, has recently noted a great number sent to America in this way from East Sussex parishes from the late 1820s to 1850. The curate of Brede put a list of those from his parish in the back of one of his registers in 1838, 'with the idea that it may be useful some years hence in tracing the relations of any person who may by industry and prudence acquire property in a foreign land'. Material about such parish-assisted emigration under the new Poor Law of 1834 is to be found in the Poor Law Union Papers in the Public Record Office. These are arranged alphabetically by counties and unions. Mr Monger quotes the example of the Aylsham Poor Law Union, Norfolk, for which lists of persons emigrating, with their occupations and destinations (mainly Canada), exist for the period 1834-1837. I do not think that these have ever been systematically explored for the names of emigrants.

Church of England lists of congregations were not often maintained, but those of the Nonconformist bodies often show movement from one congregation to another, and from congregations in this country to those abroad. Quaker records are particularly well known for this, but others often contain stray references which, if collected, would be extremely valuable. I have noticed several, for instance, in the printed Baptist registers for Nottingham. 'Bounty' schemes in America might require certificates of good character from incumbents to be supplied by those to whom land grants were given.

The correspondence relating to government-assisted passages to New South Wales in the 1830s is in the Public Record Office and a good deal of it has been indexed. That regarding Tasmania has recently been calendared in detail in *Records relating to free emigration*, published by the Archives Office of Tasmania in 1975. The emigrant to Australia, however, can often be traced by the simple use of registration records in that country. His death certificate will often show his exact place of origin in this country or his parentage, or his marriage certificate or the birth certificate of one of his children may give some of those details. Much the same applies to settlers in New Zealand and, to a much smaller extent, to the United States where the records differ greatly from state to state.

Emigrants to America since Independence may sometimes be traced back to their exact places of birth by means of the naturalisation records there. The first naturalisation act passed by Congress in 1790 provided that an alien who desired to become a citizen should apply to 'any common law court of record, in any one of the states wherein he shall have resided for the term of one year at least'. There is an index to some of these (Maine, Massachusetts, New Hampshire and Rhode Island) in the National Archives at Washington and those for Mississippi have been printed. The records of foreign Protestants naturalised in the American and West Indian Colonies between 1740 and 1776 appear in the Public Record Office and lists of them have been printed as volume 26 of the publications of the Huguenot Society of London.

In the tracing of a person who went out of this country to some place abroad it is a popular misconception that a passport was needed, will contain numerous details of great importance to the genealogist, and not least show where the holder came from in this country. The fact is of course that passports were not generally required until the First World War, although it would have been very foolish to have gone to Russia, Cuba, Portugal or Turkey without first obtaining one and having it visaed by the appropriate consul in London. As the Foreign Office Guide used to say, however, 'they are found to be convenient, as offering a ready means of identification, and more particularly when letters have to be claimed at a poste restante'. In England they could be granted 'to all persons either known to the Secretary of State or recommended to him by some person who is known to him; or upon the application of any banking firm established in London, or in any part of the United Kingdom; or upon the production of a Certificate of Identity signed by any Mayor, Magistrate, Justice of the Peace, Minister of Religion, Physician, Surgeon, Solicitor or Notary, resident in the United Kingdom'. The certificate of identity, in the wording suggested in the Foreign Office List, only gives the name and place of residence of the applicant, and a certificate of birth or baptism was only demanded in exceptional circumstances.

Such passports might be obtained abroad on application to the Consul in the foreign country to which one had gone, and details of these applications sometimes appear with the usual consular records at the Public Record Office. Those from Bavaria, for instance, exist there from 1824. This also works in reverse and a volume of 'passport letters', for instance, from the American Legation in London, 1795–1812, exists in the National Archives in Washington.

At the Public Record Office are Registers of Passports issued, showing the destination of the applicant, in chronological order from 1795 onwards. These are indexed only from 1851 to 1862 and from 1874 to 1898. The Record Office also has a collection of 1,852 representative examples of passports issued between 1809 and 1921. This collection includes some passports issued in the late eighteenth and early nineteenth centuries by Foreign Missions in this country to British subjects wishing to travel abroad. The practice of foreign countries issuing passports to the nationals of other countries ceased in 1858. Up to 1898 the passports were in the form of single sheets folded in four. From that date to 1923, when the modern book form was introduced, they were in eight-page folded 'books'.

Chapter 5

The Possibilities

The element of chance involved when tracing a pedigree is something which has to be encountered before it can be appreciated. The thoughtless death of an ancestor shortly before the first Census was taken which would have shown his birthplace, for instance, is particularly infuriating!

Success in general depends on several things. Firstly, if the surname is uncommon then identification, even over the widest areas, becomes possible. A name which is generally uncommon, however, may be particularly frequent in a limited area and thus make identification impossible unless the Christian names used in your particular family are equally unusual. Secondly, a family which remains in one place and continues in the same trade over a long period will clearly be easier to trace than one that moves about and changes its occupation. Thirdly, a professional family or one of higher social class owning property, will generally leave more record of its activities than a labouring family without property. Fourthly, the records necessary for the tracing of the family need to have been preserved, but it must be realised that their scope, quantity and survival vary considerably from place to place.

Thus a relatively humble family with a very common surname which remains in the same place may be traced three or four hundred years with relative ease whereas a more wealthy family with the same surname may not be traced even through the last century because of movement from one place to another of which no verbal tradition or documentary evidence survives within the family. It is a common fallacy that the great wealth of personal documentation required by government departments and others will make everyone easily traceable in the future. This is unfortunately far from being the case. Much is destroyed within a very short period and it has been only since 1968 that the marriage and death certificates of this country have been made to relate to those of birth. The indexes of births, marriages and deaths, however, have always been far from reliable and though there has been some improvement in their content since 1912, the general use of initials instead of second Christian names, which makes identification so much more difficult, can only be deplored.

With reasonable luck, however, and by the use of the Census returns the majority of pedigrees can be traced to about 1800. If the first census returns take one to a country area prior to that date, they may generally be taken another generation or two before difficulty occurs. If families remained in the larger towns prior to 1800 but came in from the country at some earlier date, that movement will be the stumbling block. As a result of this large numbers of pedigrees cannot be traced to 1700. The greater mobility of population in the seventeenth century and the Civil War and Commonwealth period put an end to many others, but the great 'finis' which is written across practically all the remainder comes with the mid-sixteenth century and the lack of parish registers prior to 1538. The pedigrees of those who held a certain amount of land and perhaps because of it were always in the courts may be taken further, but it is as well to remember that the great wealth of Lord Nuffield and all the genealogical expertise that he could muster could not take the ancestry of his yeoman family beyond about 1580 with certainty.

Thus it is often a matter of the greatest disappointment that an early emigrant family which has been traced to 1620 with comparative ease in New England, and whose place of origin in England has been discovered with the utmost difficulty, may then only be traced a generation or so in this country and that again in the face of many obstacles. Of families which remained in this country and had a right to arms, Sir Christopher Lynch-

Robinson, author of *Intelligible Heraldry* (1948), calculated that only about 350 have continuously held their lands in England from the reign of Henry VIII to the present time.

The possibilities are to some extent illustrated by the labouring family of Warner at Walkern in Hertfordshire. There are some problems of identification in this very prolific family with a common surname, but their use of surnames as Christian names has made it possible to trace the main lines. In the last century David Warner lived in Frog Hall Lane and was an under-gardener at the local mansion, Clay Hall (now Walkern Hall). A younger brother, Joseph, was a 'dealer in foules', and another, Daniel, worked at the brewery run by Samuel Wright. Their father Joseph Warner (1807-1836), a farm labourer, had died young and left his widow Sarah a 'cheerwoman' in the parish. He was the son of another farm labourer, Richard Harvey Warner (1765-1839), who rented a house at Walkern for £2. 15s. a year from William Andrews, a local farmer, according to the latter's account books at the County Record Office. He in turn was the son of Harvey Warner (1737–1816), the son of Francis Warner (1707–1785), a brickmaker. The latter mortgaged the two cottages he had received from his father Anthony Warner (1677–1754), another brickmaker, until he owed £93 more on them than they were worth. From endorsements on the deeds, it appears that for a further guinea paid on the day he went to Baldock Fair in 1770 he gave up his right to them to Henry Smith, a staymaker in Baldock. He was buried from the workhouse – a pretty black and white building still standing behind Trinity Church in Stevenage High Street – in 1785.

His father, Anthony, had bought the cottages for £37, prior to his marriage at Walkern in 1703.

This Anthony was the son of another Anthony Warner, buried in 1723, who was undoubtedly the son of another who had children in the parish between 1663 and 1669, and probably earlier, but there is a gap in the Parish Registers caused by the Civil War. The occupations of these earlier generations are unfortunately not known, but the first Anthony Warner had married at Ardeley, a neighbouring parish, in 1647 and was buried at Walkern in 1671. His possible further ancestry has not been searched for at Ardeley.

Harvey Warner took his name from his mother, Mary Harvey, who was buried a pauper in 1787. Her father Richard Harvey, a butcher, seems to have been the nephew of Thomas Harvey, glazier, of Walkern (who was the last witness at the trial of Jane Wenham and the son of Richard Harvey, who had been fined for not attending church and for non-payment of church rates in 1663) by Sarah Hine, whose death in 1700 was said to have followed her bewitchment by Jane Wenham. Here we are lucky, for the accounts of the trial of Jane Wenham, found guilty of conversing with the Devil in the form of a cat at Hertford Assizes in 1712 and sentenced to death – the last witch so sentenced in England – but reprieved by Queen Anne, give an extra bonus of information in that period.

An example of a less rural kind is that of the ancestry of Samuel Henry Hackney, an Independent, who was a newspaper reporter in Macclesfield and Wigan. He was born at Macclesfield in 1853, where his father, John Hackney, was a warehouseman. Although John married in the Independent chapel at Macclesfield he was baptised in the Parish Church in 1828. His father, another Henry, who died before the 1851 Census was taken, was fortunately also born in Macclesfield, in 1802. He was a silkman. The marriage of his father John Hackney, a silk throwster, could not be found at Macclesfield, but by searching the registers of neighbouring parishes it was found at Prestbury in 1790, he being described as of Macclesfield. However, John was baptised at Congleton in 1767 and his first child was baptised there in 1792. The marriage of John's father has not been found, but there seems little doubt that the father, Samuel Hackney, is the one baptised at Congleton in 1731, the son of another Samuel, a silk weaver, who married at Prestbury in 1724 describing himself as of Macclesfield where his first child was baptised. Although the name Hackney is quite common in this area the baptism of this Samuel has not been found. There is the baptism of a Samuel Hackney, son of Joseph (a shoemaker) and Martha, from Congleton, at Astbury in 1709, but he would only have been fifteen at the time of marriage. William, the shoemaker, had many children baptised at Astbury between 1689 and 1707 by a wife called Margaret who was buried in the latter year. Was Margaret also called Martha (her first child was baptised Martha in 1689), and was Samuel two or three years old when he was baptised, or did he marry at the age of fifteen? Joseph did not leave a will, and his name is not carried down in Samuel's family, which follows a quite different trade.

I cannot say in this case that all the possible sources have been consulted, but the problem which has arisen after a fair amount of research is one which many of us will encounter in some form or other during the course of our searches.

I speak of descents in England, but in Wales and Scotland, where high concentrations of certain surnames are extremely common, the problems are to that extent greater and many ancestries end in the eighteenth century. In Wales, for instance, the male line of Lord Snowdon cannot be taken beyond 1765. In Ireland the loss of records in this century is only partly compensated for by the land registry (from 1708) which did not exist in England. The tracing of an Irish family whose origins lie in England is perhaps even more difficult than that of a family which crossed the Atlantic, and the recording of the Catholics has left so much to be desired that they can rarely be taken beyond the first quarter of the last century. President Kennedy's family, for instance, goes no further than his great-grandfather who was born at Dunganstown, Co. Wexford, in 1823.

Knightly and armigerous families may be traced into the fourteenth century but beyond that only a very small minority will go. The existing body of pedigrees dating from before that date, many published in the last century, must be treated with the greatest scepticism. These older descents, largely based on inadequate evidence, wishful thinking or sheer invention, have been banished from modern editions of Burke's *Peerage* and *Landed Gentry* but they survive of course in the older editions and in other places such as the early county histories and are continually dredged up in evidence against me and will, I fear, never be laid entirely to rest.

If I say that none of the twenty-five barons who signed Magna Carta in 1215 has left descendants in the male line I shall be inundated with outraged letters, but it is of course possible to go further than that and say that the same applies to those who were at the Battle of Hastings with William I (once described in a letter I received as 'Norman the Conqueror'!). I am not denying that authentic descents exist in the male line from the Normans but only from those who are *known* to have been at the battle, for there are a certain number of such descents from persons mentioned in the Domesday Book who were probably here for the battle or arrived shortly thereafter. They can be seen to be Normans from their names but their places of origin in Normandy may well not be known.

The book *The origins of some Anglo-Norman families* by Lewis Lloyd (1951) gives details of about three hundred families whose place of origin in Normandy is known, but they are by no means all still existent in the male line. The great importance which in the past has been attached to an ancestor's having been at Hastings has bedevilled much English genealogy, and many pedigrees have been forcibly extended a few more generations to include such a one.

Walter Rye collected from six various versions of the so-called Battle Abbey Roll the names of about 1,600 people, but that Roll was probably a fourteenth-century production, is absolutely unreliable and, of course, cannot be shown to have been in the possession of the Abbey. In 1931 a French committee set up a tablet in the church at Falaise in Normandy where the Conqueror was born, containing the names of 315 people they believed to have been at the Battle of Hastings, but English historians have been more careful.

Geoffrey White, the late distinguished editor of *The Complete Peerage*, believed that only fifteen names taken from the histories of William of Poitiers and of Orderic and from the

Bayeux Tapestry could be accepted with certainty. They are Robert de Beaumont (later Earl of Leicester); Eustace, Count of Boulogne; William of Evreux; Geoffrey of Mortagne, Count of Perche; William FitzOsbern (later Earl of Hereford); Aimery, Vicomte de Thouars; Hugh de Montfort the Constable; Walter Giffard; Ralf de Tosni; Hugh de Grandmesnil; William de Warenne (later Earl of Surrey); William Malet; Turstin Fitz Rou; Engenulf de Laigle who was killed at the battle, and Odo, Bishop of Bayeux (later Earl of Kent). He accepted that four more (Robert, Count of Mortain; Geoffrey de Mowbray, Bishop of Coutances; and the vassals Wadard and Vital from Bayeux) were without doubt in the Conqueror's army and thus probably at Hastings. He had no axe to grind, and said about this list, 'I am not one of those fortunate persons descended from a gallant knight who would certainly have fought at Hastings if the pedigree-makers had invented him in time. Indeed, I might claim to be one of the few persons in England not descended (so far as I know) through the female line from William the Conqueror, although no doubt I might be deprived of that distinction any day by the researches of some too industrious genealogist.'

He later allowed the possible addition of six more names put forward by Professor D.C. Douglas, two additional names from, Orderic and four from charters (Goubert d'Auffay Robert de Vitot, Roger son of Turold, Gerelm de Panilleuse, Erchembald son of Erchembald the Vicomte, and Robert fitz Erneis), but would not allow 'the heir of Ponthieu' who is said to have been one of the four who mutilated the body of the dying Harold, or the minstrel nicknamed 'Incisor Ferri' or Taillefer who went before the Norman host and continued singing and juggling with his sword until he was slain, both mentioned in a Latin poem attributed to Guy, Bishop of Amiens. However, more recently the editors of that contemporary poem in the Oxford Medieval Texts series (1972) are inclined to think the details authentic.

Fortunately the passions which such arguments about the companions of the Conqueror used to arouse are to a large extent a thing of the past and the energies of most genealogists since the War have been devoted to much later problems.

Examples of families with a direct male descent from Domesday tenants are Fitzgerald (including amongst them the Dukes of Leinster and Marquesses of Lansdowne) and Carew of Devon and Cornwall, both descending from Walter Fitz-Other, the castellan of the castle at Windsor. Gresley of Drakelowe in Derbyshire, descending from Nigel de Stafford is another, and perhaps also St John. From sub-tenants mentioned in Domesday descend Shirley and Wrottesley. The Shirley family (which may not be of Norman origin) are probably unique in that they held Ettington in Derbyshire in 1086 and own it still. The Malet family, of which the present head is Sir Edward Malet, may descend from the above-mentioned William Malet who was at Hastings but the line put forward by Col. G. E. G. Malet in *The Genealogists Magazine* in 1939 and shown in Burke's *Peerage* is unfortunately by no means proven.

Of course there were some families in England before the Normans came! Descents from these are perhaps of greater interest, and although from the evidence of their names there are several early families which must have had an English ancestry, in the opinion of Sir Anthony Wagner the descents of only two have been proved from pre-Conquest Englishmen, Arden and Berkeley. Aelfwine was Sheriff of Warwickshire before the Conquest and his son Turchil was a great Domesday tenant. The latter's son, Siward of Arden, was deprived of much of his land by William Rufus but his descendants held property in Warwickshire until 1643 and several younger lines flourish now in Australia, the present head of the family in England being Dr George Philip Arden (bn. 1913) of Virginia Water, Surrey, who is 27th in descent from the Sheriff. It was to the Warwickshire branch of this family that Mary Arden, the mother of William Shakespeare, probably belonged.

The Berkeley family of Berkeley Castle in Gloucestershire descend in the male line from Robert FitzHarding, a Bristol merchant who is thought to have been the grandson of Eadnoth Staller, an officer in the household of Edward the Confessor, but the identifications are not proven.

Other families descending from twelfth-century Englishmen are the Stanleys, Earls of Derby (at Stanley in Staffordshire); the Lumleys, Earls of Scarborough (at Lumley in Co. Durham); the Earls Fitzwilliam (from Hopton in Yorkshire); and the Asshetons (at Ashton under Lyne).

Elsewhere in the British Isles ancient descents are not unknown. In Ireland descents from the fifth century may rest upon lost written records incorporated in later writings, but beyond that are the subject of much dispute. If authentic, these descents may be the longest in Western Europe. Niall of the Nine Hostages, high king of Ireland, lived at the end of the fourth century and died, according to various computations, between about 405 and 427. Several descents from him to the present in the male line and running through fifty generations are printed in Burke's *Peerage* in the account of the family of Lord O'Neill but one at least according to R. S. Lea in the *Complete Peerage* 'does not bear examination', whilst Lord O'Neill is himself by male descent a Chichester. Niall may have had a brother, Brion, the father of King Daui Galach who died in 502 and was the ancestor of The O'Conor Don through the Kings of Connaught. The present Lord Inchiquin undoubtedly descends in the male line through the Princes of Thomond from Brian Boru, Ireland's greatest king, who was assassinated in 1014. From Mary, a sister of the first Earl of Inchiquin, who married Michael Boyle, Archbishop of Armagh, descends Queen Elizabeth the Queen Mother. Gospatric, the Earl of Northumberland under William the Conqueror, descended from the hereditary abbots of Dunkeld who were probably of the kin of St Columba, the great-grandson of Niall who founded the abbey of Iona in the seventh century. From him undoubtedly descends the baronetical family of Dunbar of Mochrum and perhaps the great English family of Neville of Raby now represented by the Marquess of Abergavenny, all again in the male line.

The royal house of Scotland was founded by Fergus Mor MacEirc who came from County Antrim and died about 501, but his male descendants came to an end with the death of Malcolm II in 1034. All the later Scottish kings descend from him in the female line, however, and there are numerous descents in England stemming from the marriage of Matilda, the daughter of Malcolm III, to Henry I of England. The present heads of practically all the present and former ruling houses of Europe from Russia to Albania and from the Scandinavian countries to Monaco descend from Fergus's descendant, King James II of Scotland, who died in 1460.

Rhodri Mawr, the King of Gwynned, unified most of Wales and died in 878. He was descended from Cunedda (and the latter's father-in-law, the semi-historical Coel Hen Godebog or Coel the Old) who came to Gwynned about 450 and whose ancestry for a further three generations may well be authentic, and male descents from him are claimed by several Welsh families including those of Anwyl of Lligwy, Co. Merioneth, and Williams-Ellis of Glasfryn, Co. Caernarvon. Female descents from Rhodri Mawr are legion.

Geoffrey of Monmouth about 1135, recording descents fabricated at least as early as the ninth century, takes the ancestry of Rhodri Mawr back to Noah through Brutus, a grandson of Aeneas, and through the Kings of Troy, Hector and Priam. This descent, together with that of the Anglo-Saxon monarchs including Alfred the Great through the storm-god Woden back to Sceaf the son of Noah, who is said by Bede in his *Ecclesiastical History* to have been born in the Ark was put together with other fabulous descents in a large sheet pedigree compiled by G. M. H. Milner and published in 1923. This worthless pedigree, *The illustrious lineage of the royal house of Britain*, has gone through many editions obtaining a wide circulation, and derives David, Prince of Wales (later Edward VIII and Duke of Windsor), from David and the Royal House of Judah.

Unfortunately no male line descents from the Saxon kings exist, but the ancestry of Alfred has been carried by females into great numbers of English and foreign families. This brings us to female descents in general. Through them, and through the 'gateway ancestors' that lead to them, even the humblest amongst us can aspire, if that is the correct word, to descents of incredible length. Such descents are, however, undoubtedly shared by many hundreds of thousands of people and are far from being unique. The acreage of paper devoted to their repetition in many a family history, however, confirms the wide interest they apparently hold.

The fluid nature of English society and intermarriage through diverse social classes over a long period has brought a fine trickle of royal blood to many an ordinary Englishman quite unaware of the fact. The Marquis of Ruvigny calculated that by 1911 King Edward III of England probably had upwards of a hundred thousand descendants, half that number stemming from his eldest son Lionel, Duke of Clarence. The number must be much greater now. In 1903 the living descendants of Mary, Queen of Scots, numbered 1,440: now it is 10,534. In legitimate lines the latter is almost completely royal and foreign. Illegitimate lines from Charles II and William IV amongst others however, add considerably to this total and are predominantly English. Charles II by Nell Gwynn, for example, has fifteen hundred living descendants, including some like the Duchess of Portland and Lady Delamere who descend from other mistresses as well.

Beyond Edward III the royal blood flows out in England through Edmund Crouchback the son of Henry III, through Thomas of Brotherton and Edmund of Woodstock the younger sons of Edward I and their sisters Joan and Elizabeth, through Eleanor the daughter of King John, and through illegitimate lines like those from Robert, Earl of Gloucester, the bastard of Henry I.

Sir Anthony Wagner has shown how particular descendants of these have acted as gateways to royal ancestry in particular areas of the country. The marriage, for instance, of Edward I's granddaughter Margaret de Bohun to Sir Hugh Courtenay takes his blood to many West Country families. The best example may, however, be Katheryn of Berain who died in 1591, the granddaughter of Henry VII's bastard Sir Roland Velville, 'whose progeny in North Wales by three of her four husbands was so great that she was known as Mam Cymru, the mother of Wales'. They included Dr Johnson's Mrs Thrale. The story is told of Katheryn de Berain that at her first husband's funeral her future third husband proposed to her on the way out from church, to be told that she had accepted her second on the way in, but that if he was about when she buried the second – which he was – she would marry him then!

It will come as no surprise, therefore, that every Queen Consort of England for the last seven hundred years has been descended from both William the Conqueror and Alfred the Great, or that when Anthony Armstrong-Jones married Princess Margaret he was found to have been descended – almost entirely in the female line – from Edward I. Similarly, when Captain Mark Phillips married Princess Anne the genealogists found his descent from the same king; a descent shared with Virginia Woolf and George Orwell, with Sir Billy Butlin and Neville Chamberlain, with Somerset Maugham and E. M. Forster, with Fletcher Christian the leader of the mutineers on the *Bounty*, with Lawrence of Arabia and Vaughan Williams, with George Washington the first President of the United States and with at least nineteen settlers in New England before 1650.

Naomi Mitchison descends from King John, and Franklin D. Roosevelt from Henry II (a descent he shared with Hermann Goering and possibly General de Gaulle). Sir Winston Churchill had a descent from Henry VII, and Jenny, the wife of Karl Marx, from David I of Scotland! However, the descents of other American presidents as given in Burke's *Presidential Families of the United States of America* (1975) – of Abraham Lincoln from Edward I, of Richard M. Nixon from Edward III, and of Ulysses S. Grant from David I of Scotland – have all been rejected as unacceptable by American genealogists.

The late Mr Raymond Berthon of Selsey, Sussex, a member of the Society of Genealogists, and a man of much foreign ancestry, was descended in more than seven hundred different ways from Henry II.

Thus although the direct male line of one's ancestry may not go very far, it is by tracing all the female lines that links of this kind are found in so many families. Practically everyone has 'one good line' and many if they search far enough will find several. The Society of Genealogists asks its members to file details of their immediate ancestors on forms called 'birth briefs' which show all their sixteen great-great-grandparents. It is surprising how difficult it is to complete such a form (in a random sample of fifty filed I found only four were complete) even after extensive research, but the completion of the cross-word becomes almost obsessive and once done the effort may well transfer itself to completing the thirty-two great-great-great-grandparents, and so on, 64, 128, 256, 512 etc. Special books have been designed for recording this sort of information, that by William H. Whitmore called *Ancestral Tablets*, first published at Boston, Massachusetts, in 1885, having space for 128. The more recent design by J. S. Gordon Clark called *A Family Tree Album* allows the pedigree to be continued beyond 128 in appendixes. Vast fan-shaped and circular charts are also published but have obviously less space for recording the details. They have a wide circulation in America and have been popular on the Continent for some time but have been little used in England.

However, the attempt of Lt.-Col. W. H. Turton to trace all the ancestors of Elizabeth the daughter of Edward IV in *The Plantagenet Ancestry* (1928) is an important exception. At a lower level the late Bethel G. Bouwens, *A Thousand Ancestors* (1935) is a notable example.

George Watson attempted the 4096 quarters of Edward VII but Queen Victoria let the side down and only mustered 255 out of her 256. More recently Gerald Paget has attempted the 262,144 quarters of the Prince of Wales, but about forty thousand have been left untraced. George Watson also provided the sixteen quarters of the English queen consorts in a series of articles in *The Genealogist*, but these are now superseded by Paget's work, and Sir Anthony Wagner did the same for the sixty-four quarters of Queen Elizabeth the Queen Mother in *The Genealogists' Magazine* in 1940, providing 44 of the total, the sixteen quarters being complete. This has not been bettered by Gerald Paget, who casts doubt on one identity but is able to add another.

The term 'quarters' or 'quartiers' was formerly associated with continental notions of nobility, all the sixteen great-great-grandparents or *seize quartiers* having had a right to bear arms, but in England there are very few with such backgrounds, and even fewer with *trente-deux quartiers* where all thirty-two are armigerous.

A. C. Fox-Davies made many futile trials in order to find an existing British example of sixteen quarters when writing his *Complete Guide to Heraldry* before coming up with the late 7th Duke of Leinster, and the only authentic case of thirty-two that he had come across was that of Alfred Joseph, Lord Mowbray, Segrave and Stourton, who died in 1893. The *seize quartiers* of the 8th Duke of Buccleuch are pleasingly illustrated in *Simple Heraldry* (1952) by Sir Iain Moncreiffe and Don Pottinger.

Continental genealogists have been compiling tables of this kind since Eyzinger published his *Thesaurus Principum* in 1591. In Germany in particular there has been a systematic attempt to publish the total ancestries of celebrated persons and two volumes appeared in 1939 and 1942 under the auspices of the Third Reich. The same ideology prompted the publication of six fat volumes of *Ahnentafeln berühmter Deutscher* (1929–44), which include the ancestries of people like Hitler, Goering and Hess, Goethe and Schiller, Kant, Wagner, Liebig and Zeppelin.

These studies particularly appealed to Otto Forst de Battaglia and in his *Traité de Généalogie* (1949) he comments on the published works in some detail and gives interesting comparative details of the results of cousin marriages in tables of this kind.

When first cousins marry and have children, those children have only six great-grandparents instead of the normal eight. In the same way Alphonso XIII of Spain had only 111 ancestors where but for cousin marriages he would normally have had 1024, the Count of Paris has 546 instead of 8192, and the Archduke Francis Ferdinand of Austria, whose assassination 'started' the First World War, had 4200 instead of 65,536.

Forst de Battaglia thought that the record lay with Antiochus X Eusebius, King of Syria, who died in 92 B.C., and who as a result of brother-sister marriages had only 24 ancestors where any normal person would have had 256 and where even Alphonso XIII had 51. It seems to me, however, that these figures could be bettered as the result of brother-sister and uncle-niece marriages amongst the ancestors of Queen Cleopatra Berenice of Egypt. She was the wife and step-mother of Ptolemy XI, the last legitimate male of the dynasty, until he murdered her nineteen days after their wedding. In both cases, however, there are problems and the exact number of ancestors cannot be determined with certainty.

Forst de Battaglia illustrates the point further with an extraordinary table showing the various lines of Henry IV, King of France, born in 1553, who by a series of cousin marriages descends from seven of the children of John II, King of France, who died in 1364. Our own Prince of Wales has, over a much longer period, twenty-two different descents from Mary, Queen of Scots, and Prince Francis of Orleans has 114!

A by-product of these studies has been the compilation of descents through the female line only, naturally an extremely difficult task, but – as it is said to be a wise man who knows his own father – perhaps resulting in a line about which there is a minimum of doubt! The longest such line must be that of Queen Victoria (shared by her descendants in the female line the Kaiser, Lord Mountbatten, and the Duke of Edinburgh) which by chance in earlier generations is also that of Charles II, of the Young Pretender and of Catherine II of Russia.

This goes back, not as Forst de Battaglia thought to a Mongolian Princess of the Kumans, but through 28 generations (from Queen Victoria) to one Erembourg, the wife of Gervase de Château-du-Loire in the eleventh century. A matrilineal descent from Kuthen, Khan of the Kumans, however, still remains for Philippa of Hainault, the wife of Edward III. The matrilineal descent of the present Queen has not, so far as I am aware, been taken beyond Frances Webb of Oaksey, Wiltshire, who married Thomas Salisbury at Salisbury Cathedral in 1795.

The person who appears most at the head of genealogies in western Europe is undoubtedly Charlemagne, the Emperor of the West, who died in 814. (Forst de Battaglia calculated that he probably has twenty million living descendants, including all those descended from the English Kings above mentioned.) As a result of this, considerable interest has attached itself to his ancestry and it is through him that more than one has looked for ancestries going back into the ancient world. They have not had much success and an ancient pedigree which derived his known ancestor St Arnulf, Bishop of Metz, who died in 640, from the Merovingian King Chlotar I (died 561) and Tonantius Ferreolus, Roman consul in 453, and the latter's grandfather Afranius Syagrius, consul in 382, has generally been rejected by modern scholars. However, Professor David H. Kelley of Calgary has suggested that this pedigree may have been that of Arnoald, another Bishop of Metz, whose granddaughter may have married St Arnulf's son.

Descents from the ancient world not being found in the Gallo-Roman areas of continuity, they have been searched for on the fringes of the Roman Empire, in Spain through the Moors, in the Eastern Empire, and in Armenia and Georgia.

The marriage of Edmund, Duke of York, the son of Edward III, to Isabel the daughter of Pedro III, King of Castile, was long thought to have brought the blood of the family of the prophet Mohammed into many English families. Along with all the royal families of Europe she descends from Alfonso VI, King of Castile. It was thought that the descent came through his wife Elizabeth, before baptism called Zaïda, the daughter of Mohammed II, the Moslem King of Seville, who died in 1095, and who was himself descended from Ittaf ibn Naim who came to Spain from Arabia in 741 and who may have belonged to the family of the kings of Hira. Unfortunately this descent has recently been proved baseless, and Zaïda, whose parentage is unknown, was not the mother of the daughter from whom the descent comes.

Isabel of Castile, however, possibly had another Moslem descent through Ramiro II of Leon from Musa el Bekra, the Arab conqueror of Northern Africa in 699–709 and of Spain in 712, and the possible descent of the wives of Edward I and Henry III of England from the Moslem family of Banu Qasi, lords of Saragossa in the eighth and ninth centuries, and its relationship to the Caliphs of Cordoba has been explored by Professor C. J. Jacobs but cannot be taken beyond the early ninth century. Such a descent, however, gives a possible Moorish ancestry to a wide range of families in England and America but cousinships to the Agha Khan and the King of Jordan, and to other descendants of the family of the Prophet, such as Haroun al Raschid of *Arabian Nights* fame, have yet to be established.

According to Forst de Battaglia a similarly remote cousinship existed between Kang-Té (perhaps better known as Pou-yi), the puppet Emperor of Manchuria and the heir of the last imperial dynasty of China, and many western families. He descended in the female line from Genghis Khan, who through Anne the wife of Prince Feodor Rostislavitch (died 1299) of the Russian royal house of Rurik was said to be the ancestor of the Romanovs, but this descent does not stand up to more modern criticism. A later 'lateral' link with China has, however, been noted, for in 1270 the nephew (Charles II, King of Naples) of Henry III's queen married the sister-in-law of an Emperor of Byzantium (Andronicus II Palaeologus) whose half-sister had five years previously married the nephew of Kublai Khan, Emperor of China! The latter was the grandson of Genghis Khan.

In the Eastern Empire the search for long pedigrees has not on the whole been successful and although connections with the imperial families have been found it has not been possible to take the ancestries very far. Through Stephen V, King of Hungary, the queen of Edward III had a descent from Theodore Lascaris, Emperor of the East, but no line of his ancestry can be taken beyond the ninth century with certainty. Theophano, the wife of the Emperor Otto II and ancestress of Edward I is by tradition thought to have been the daughter of the Byzantine Emperor Romanus II (died 963), but her origin is much disputed.

For some time attention has been given to descents through to the ancient world in Georgia and Armenia, based to a large extent on the work of Prince Cyril Toumanoff of Princeton. In *Blood Royal*, published in 1956, the authors included the outline of a descent of the Duke of Edinburgh, suggested by the Prince, from Mithridates I, Shah of Persia and King of Babylon, through Guaram III, Prince of Iberia, from whom the Bagratid Kings of Georgia traced a descent. The blood descent of the Duke, however, may be lost through the Romanovs, as the father of Tsar Paul may have been Prince Saltykov and not Tsar Peter III.

This possible descent receives little attention in a much more detailed account of those lines in 'Bridges to Antiquity', a section of Sir Anthony Wagner's *Pedigree and Progress* (1975), where, relying again on Prince Toumanoff, a descent of seventy-three generations from Pharnabazus I, King of Iberia (roughly the same territory as modern Georgia), born in the time of Alexander the Great, to Queen Elizabeth II is given. The descent, which is extremely problematic, passed through the Arsacid, Gregorid, Mamikonid, Bagratid, Artsuni, Pahlavid and Rubenid dynasties, and the d'Iselin and Lusignan families, to Anne of Cyprus the wife of Louis, Duke of Savoy, a great-great-great-grandmother of both Mary, Queen of Scots, and Henry IV of France. It is thus with truth that Prince Dolgorouky said that the origin of the Georgian princes was 'lost in the night of time'.

Chapter 6

Forgery and Deception

It has often been said that few genealogists are deliberately fraudulent but that many through lack of general competence and ability put together family histories that would not stand up to any critical examination. However, there are always those who, having traced their pedigrees as far as their competence or the availability of records will take them, seek to extend them further by other means. After all, the first thing that a client asks a professional genealogist is, 'How far have you traced *your* family?', and if the answer to that seems unsatisfactory the client will not be very impressed by the professional's general ability. That he 'improves' his own pedigree, however, does not mean that he will not be critical of his work for others or of other genealogies.

The history of English antiquarianism is rich in curious examples of this self-deception. The great Marquis de Ruvigny who died in 1921 was well known as the author of five volumes enumerating the descendants of King Edward III and of *The Jacobite Peerage*, but his use of that title seems to have been based on a seventeenth-century marriage which did not take place. Sir Egerton Brydges, an extremely able genealogist who produced the 1812 and final edition of *Collins's Peerage* on which the pedigrees in Burke's Peerage were based, claimed the Barony of Chandos and made a perfect nuisance of himself through twelve years of legal proceedings although his whole claim was based on a false entry he had inserted in the parish registers of Maidstone. George Harrison, better known as General Plantagenet-Harrison, who spent almost thirty years in the Public Record Office laboriously extracting material for a monumental *History of Yorkshire*, printed in the only volume of it to be published in 1879 a fantastic pedigree showing a descent in the male line from the god Odin. He claimed on little evidence to be Duke of Lancaster, passing over his elder brother who would in any case have had a prior claim, because he was, as he told Paley Baildon, 'a damned fool'! He was not, however, 'an entirely fictitious personage' as G. S. H. L. Washington sought to show in the equally fantastic *Prince Charlie and The Bonapartes* (1960).

George Plantagenet-Harrison also had an unfortunate effect on his friends. In 1877 he encouraged the Revd John Swale, O.S.B., of Birtley in Durham, to place a notice in *The Times* in which he said that he considered it 'a sacred duty which I owe to the memory of my ancestors, and for the future benefit and welfare of my family to assume and take unto myself . . . the title of a Baronet'. He claimed to be descended from Solomon Swale who had been made a Baronet by Charles II, having whilst Member of Parliament for Aldborough in 1660 proposed the restoration of the King, a claim unfortunately unsupported by any evidence. The assumption was continued by his younger brother and nephew down to about 1920. Another Catholic friend, a naval architect called Henry de Burgh Lawson, to whom Plantagenet-Harrison dedicated his *History of Yorkshire*, also assumed an old baronetcy that year. This one was generally thought to have become extinct in 1834, but his sons continued the assumption into this century. The position was further complicated for them in 1907 when another claimant came forward, John Lawson, the Master of Whitby Union Workhouse! None of these claims, criticised in published works almost from the first day they were made, has ever been substantiated.

In the 1820s William Paver, son of a working blacksmith in York and clerk to a law stationer, obtained a position in the York probate registry. Having done some work on the history of his own family in York he early conceived the notion that he was the senior representative of the ancient house of Percy and coheir of the Baronies of Percy and Poynings through Lady Elizabeth Woodroffe, eldest daughter of the seventh Earl of Northumberland. He had christened his son, born in 1829, Percy Woodroffe Paver. In order to substantiate the claim he inserted among the genuine wills at York two fabricated wills, 'Maximilian Woodrove' (1652) and 'John Paver' (1721). The latter, a truly remarkable will, but a clumsy forgery, recited eight generations of the fictional family history. The fraud was discovered, apparently quite by chance, by a barrister searching there in 1850 and given publicity in Charles Dickens' popular magazine *Household Words*. The wills were removed and Paver was dismissed. Nothing daunted he obtained the post of Registrar of Births, Deaths and Marriages at York whilst continuing to work as a professional genealogist. According to Elvin's *Handbook of Mottoes*, published in 1860, he used the quite extraordinary motto 'Faded, but not destroyed', and it is quite clear that in spite of the open criticism of his 'fictitious pretensions' in the periodical *Herald and Genealogist* at that time he and his son Percy were doing quite well as professional genealogists, conducting a wide correspondence, particularly in America. A list of the Yorkshire pedigrees in his possession was published in 1857 in the *New England Register* and he offered copies of them at a dollar a generation. He is now chiefly remembered for his extensive and valuable abstracts from the since destroyed Yorkshire Marriage Licences, 1567-1714, which are in the British Library and have been published by the Yorkshire Archaeological Society.

William Paver's claim to the Percy descent had been taken up by another eccentric genealogist, 'Sir' Thomas Christopher Banks, in his *Baronia Anglica Concentrata* (1844). Banks described Paver as 'the humble and depressed first coheir of the unhappy Earl Thomas' though 'possessing the honour of priority of blood over the present bearer of the ancient dignities', castigating the latter as 'the pompous occupier of Northumberland House and Alnwick Castle'. Banks must have forgotten that in an earlier work, his *Stemmata Anglica*, he had perversely endeavoured to back up the claim to the earldom by one James Percy, a Dublin trunkmaker, which, after many years' investigation, had been dismissed by the House of Lords in 1689 as that of 'the false and impudent pretender to the Earldom of Northumberland'.

However, where Banks was concerned, as the *Dictionary of National Biography* says, 'there was scarcely any genealogical will-of-the-wisp which he was not ready, if the fancy struck him, to adopt as a reality', and although he published a series of pamphlets in support of spurious claims to peerages from his 'Dormant Peerage Office' some of his published works possess a high degree of merit and reflect an enormous and painstaking industry. He is best known for his four-volume *Dormant and Extinct Baronage of England*.

In 1830 he undertook the case of Alexander Humphrys, who had laid claim to the Earldom of Stirling with a view to obtaining the vast tracts of land in Canada and the United States originally granted to the first Earl of Stirling in 1621 and to his son in 1635. Banks went to America and Ireland in search of evidence and in accordance with rights conferred on the first earl by King James I the claimant created him a Baronet of Nova Scotia and endowed him with sixteen thousand acres of non-existent land there. Humphrys, having received some recognition in Scotland, immediately offered for sale a million acres 'of most excellent land in New Brunswick'! When the documents on which he founded his claims were discovered to be forgeries, Banks ceased to make use of the title he had been given but seems generally to have been known by it. He was in his ninetieth year when he died at Greenwich in 1854. According to the *Complete Peerage* the forged documents, which were cleverly executed, were probably the work of Mademoiselle Le Normand, a well-known Parisian fortune-teller and an intimate friend of Humphrys' Italian wife.

In view of his own activities it is perhaps not surprising that Banks' *Baronia Anglica* contains a bitter attack on the professional genealogists at the College of Arms, which he variously calls the College of Mystification and the College of

Absolute Wisdom and Exclusive Knowledge, reminding it forcibly of William Radclyffe and, with much less justice, of Sir William Dethick. William Radclyffe of Darley Hall, Yorkshire, had been appointed Rouge Croix Pursuivant of Arms at the College of Arms in 1803. Eleven years later he registered there a pedigree showing his descent from the Earls of Derwentwater. Suspicions having been aroused, the descent was found to be based on a false marriage which he had inserted in the Parish Registers of Ravensfield, Yorkshire, before he came to the College, and on a variety of other fabrications. He was prosecuted for forgery, fined £50 and sentenced to three months' imprisonment at the York Assizes in 1820, but he did not resign his appointment until 1823. He had been an active genealogist specialising in the pedigrees of Yorkshire families and had been much used by other Yorkshire genealogists. I do not know if there is evidence that he tampered with the pedigrees of other people but he used his own to good effect and on the strength of the Derwentwater descent and the connection it gave to King Edward VI he succeeded in obtaining the admission of his younger brother to Christ's Hospital as being of kin to the founder. He had failed, however, in a similar attempt to obtain a beneficial lease from Greenwich Hospital of a considerable estate which had belonged to his alleged ancestors.

The attack by Banks on Sir William Dethick, a sixteenth-century Garter King of Arms, resulted from his assigning the arms of Lord Grey of Ruthin to George Rotherham in a pedigree 'corruptly' concocted in 1594. Many charges have been laid at this turbulent and arrogant man's door but he was perhaps the most skilful herald of his day. That he claimed to be descended from the family of Dethick of Dethick Hall in Derbyshire when in fact his grandfather was a Dutch or German yeoman armourer almost goes without saying. He courageously proclaimed Essex a traitor and when at his trial the Earl said that he had seen no herald he was told 'an herald, though a wicked man, is nevertheless a herald'.

The Kentish antiquary Sir Edward Dering who invented a

Saxon descent for himself in the seventeenth century went to the lengths of having brasses engraved for his pseudo ancestors and placed in Pluckley church. In this century it is perhaps not so easy to get away with this sort of thing, but a gentleman presently living on the Isle of Wight in attempts to bolster his claim to an ancient foreign title recently went to considerable lengths to drop false documents amongst others more authentic in several county record offices. Fortunately these rather obvious cuckoos have been found in their nests and removed. At the Public Record Office I am told that he was a little more lucky, a false sheet he had left there being stamped and bound in with others before being noticed! Another gentleman living abroad but of English ancestry, a very able genealogist in his own right, recently submitted a pedigree of his family to Burke's Peerage Ltd for publication in the *Landed Gentry* which because of its particularly interesting nature was investigated and found to be almost entirely fictitious, the truth being extremely colourful but not at all of the social level generally to be found in the pages of the *Landed Gentry*.

These have all been fairly harmless cases of self-deception, except perhaps when documents have been tampered with. Others, however, where a financial interest has been involved, have had a less pleasant outcome. When the seventy-nine-year-old Richard Harrison died at Warrington in 1863 he left a personal estate valued at about £100,000 and property bringing in £800 a year. He had, to his knowledge, no near relatives, and not making a will used to say that those who wanted his property could fight for it after he had gone. This they did for the next twenty-three years, and the competition was so great that before the case was settled at least fifty fictitious entries had been inserted in the registers of at least four parishes (mainly at Preston), others altered and erased, the bishop's transcripts of them similarly altered or ruthlessly destroyed, and marriage licence bonds forged, by two of the claimants.

Where the Tracy peerage was concerned the claimant James Tracy went to the added lengths of having entirely false tombstones carved and fired to make them appear old, a deception that was discovered when his claim came before the Committee for Privileges in 1847. The actual stones, which were 'planted' at Castlebrack in Ireland, were brought over and now reside in the Victoria Tower at the House of Lords with the other records of the case.

Genealogists working for their clients are open to greater temptation. It is popularly believed that they will spin out any particular piece of research and make as much from it as may be. Having found a marriage, for instance, in Boyd's Marriage Index at the Society of Genealogists, a source quite unlikely to be known to his client, the unscrupulous professional may continue his 'searches' for the marriage until the client's funds seem exhausted, when it will, as if by miracle, be produced as an inducement to the commissioning of further work. The report in one such case I saw recently said, 'We searched numerous incumbencies and other sources until we eventually ascertained that he married at St George's Hanover Square in 1833', an entry clearly obtained from Boyd's Index.

Herbert Davies, a young man engaged in 1895 by Colonel Shipway to trace his pedigree in Gloucestershire records saw his salary of 6s. a day (with an extra 35s. a week for cycle hire) likely to come rapidly to an end and as an inducement to further commissions took to forgery in a large way. He altered parish registers, substituted forged wills for others in three different probate registries, excavated the churchyard and chancel at Mangotsfield providing false identities for a lead coffin and an old effigy which he found (during the excavation of the former a labourer was injured by the fall of a stone and subsequently died), and even carved a 'sixteenth-century' inscription on a beam in the belfry, altogether spending about £700 of the Colonel's money before being discovered. This gentleman, who gave interviews to the press as the 'Principal Genealogical Specialist', received three years' hard labour at the Central Criminal Court in 1897.

Another who saw how the desire of the genealogist for a slightly longer pedigree could be exploited was William

Sidney Spence. Operating from Birkenhead in the 1840s he claimed to have been engaged to go through the papers left by a former Mayor of Chester, Sir John Cotgreave, and to have found therein particulars of various ancient families together with their Arms which he offered to their descendants for a fee. This false information was certified by Lady Cotgreave, who, unbeknown to the recipients, was his sister. When in 1854 Mr R. W. Dixon, J.P., of Seaton Carew, wrote to *Notes & Queries* about the five generations of his own family which he had purchased from Spence an extraordinary number of other correspondents came forward to say that they had been duped in the same way. Doubtless there were many others but the victims either did not care to publicise their gullibility or did not know they had been taken in.

Another trick of the fraudulent genealogist has been to issue prospectuses for books on the history of particular families, to collect subscriptions, and then not to produce the books. The firm of Janson & Co. was severely castigated for so doing in *Truth* on 8th March, 1933, and I have known other more recent examples. About the same time a Mr Bolton in Birmingham collected small amounts of money from members of the Society of Genealogists living abroad (clearly taking their names from the *Genealogists' Magazine*) for old deeds he did not have to sell; and 'Sir John Brunton', who did not exist, operating as the Secretary of the Faculty of Genealogy Research at an accommodation address in Conduit Street, London, was selling for £4 or twenty dollars 'an exact reproduction, handmade, large size, in full oil colors, on parchment, framed and glassed' the arms of any 'Family name crest' in the worst but never-failing traditions of the heraldic stationer.

In view of this general background it is perhaps not surprising that there have always been those who employ two professional genealogists at the same time, in the belief, I suppose, that if they are lucky one if not the other will come up with the correct ancestry and not at the same time take their patrons for a ride.

Chapter 7

The right to Arms

Those who do not already know something about their pedigrees probably do not have any right to ancestral arms. Names do not have arms. Individuals have the right to use a coat of arms if they are descended in the direct, legitimate, male line from someone whose right to those arms, by grant or descent, has been proved to the satisfaction of the Kings of Arms. In Scotland that descent must also be registered, and it is preferable that it is in England as well. No one can discover whether they have such an ancestral right to arms unless they undertake genealogical research and examine the official records.

For many years, indeed since the Civil War, and particularly in the last century and since 1945, there have been heraldic stationers, now often found in boutiques in the major department stores and on railway stations, which for a small fee will produce arms for anyone. The purveyors cover themselves nowadays by saying that there are 'No genealogical representations intended or implied'. What they are really saying, as the *Heraldry Gazette* has pointed out is, 'This coat of arms is to be found in an unreliable reference book as having once been borne by a family with your surname. The chances of the arms being genuine are about one in five; the chances of the arms, if genuine, being yours are roughly one in a hundred.'

A few years ago the purveyors of these bogus arms did not bother to cover themselves at all, and in the 1860 edition of Walford's *County Families*, for instance, amongst advertisements for 'Glenfield Patent Starch, used in the Royal Laundry' and 'Hopgood and Co.'s Celebrated Nutritive and Sedative Hair Cream' you will find, 'For Family Arms, Crest, or Pedigree, Send Name and County, and in Three Days you will receive a Correct copy of your ARMORIAL BEARINGS, Plain sketch, 3s.; in Heraldic Colours, 6s.', and 'For Correct Family Arms, Crests, etc., send Name, and County, and Fee (7s. 6d.), and in a few days you will receive a neat drawing in Heraldic Colours'. In order to confuse themselves with the College of Arms, or Heralds College as it was often then called, the firms placing these advertisements called themselves the 'Royal Heraldic Office' (T. Colleton) 'City Herald' (J. Lock) and 'The Heraldic Office' (T. Moring). Now under the heading 'Send Us Your Name for Your Own Personal Coat of Arms', we are told 'The Art of Heraldry is put to work on your name and after extensive investigation, your personal Coat of Arms is put into sculptured brass, mounted on a solid wood plaque'.

The source of instant arms used by generations of these stationers has been Sir John Bernard Burke's *General armory: the general armory of England, Scotland, Ireland and Wales, comprising a registry of armorial bearings from the earliest to the present time*, earlier published as *The Encyclopedia of Heraldry*, of which his last edition appeared in 1884. It contains a hundred thousand descriptions of arms in alphabetical order by surname, taken from every conceivable source, thousands of which are bogus, incorrectly blazoned (or described) or wrongly attributed. No source is included for any of the information given. In a recent American bibliography of books on heraldry and genealogy Burke's *General Armory* is described as 'Indispensable for the librarian because, although in many cases the American researcher is not really entitled to the arms, it answers most questions'. Unfortunately, it is not only the American researcher who is 'not really entitled to the arms'!

Burke's *Armory* was to a large extent based on the earlier work of William Berry, *Encyclopaedia heraldica* (4 vols, 1828-1840), which in turn derived from Joseph Edmondson's *A complete body of heraldry* (2 vols, 1780). This latter work contains about fifty thousand arms and was the compilation of the Mowbray Herald Extraordinary, being based largely on the work of John Anstis, the great eighteenth-century Garter King at Arms, and a considerable scholar. It is always instructive to check back in these two works any entry found in Burke's *Armory*. If the heraldic stationers cannot find what they want they turn to the continental equivalent of Burke's *Armory*, Johannes B. Rietstap's *Armorial General* (2 vols, 1887) in the hope that something can be found there. As a result of such a search we found in a recent investigation that the Yorkshire family of Falkingham had been given the arms of the German chief of the General Staff in the First World War, Erich von Falkenhayn, no entry being found under Falkingham in Burke.

Is it to be wondered at, therefore, that many people cherish representations of what they believe to be their family arms, or crests, and that they think that these will be the talisman or key to unlock all the secrets of their family history? A steady stream of them goes to the College of Arms in London, but as the present Garter King of Arms has said, 'It comes as a disappointment to them to learn that, while it may be possible to trace the origin of the coat of arms in question, and particulars of the person to whom it was first granted, allowed or confirmed by the Heralds, this will not necessarily throw any direct light on their own pedigree'. The inquirer will be told that the arms were granted, say, to John Scobell of Plymouth in 1629, to be used by himself and his descendants, and he will reply that his name is Scobell and that his family has always used these arms, and that he must therefore be descended from John Scobell. 'It naturally follows,' he will say, 'that there is only a "gap" in my pedigree, and that by working down from John Scobell and backwards from myself, this gap will be closed.'

'Unhappily,' as Garter says, 'experience shows that in this Vale of Tears the facts are otherwise'. Only too often investigation of Mr Scobell's pedigree will show that he is in no way related to John Scobell of Plymouth, and in consequence has no right whatever to the arms which have for so long adorned his parlour, and which, as he can show, were already when Queen Victoria came to the throne used on the seal of his grandfather, a man of unblemished reputation. That honest, but ignorant, man, like thousands of others, had sent his 3s. for a Plain Sketch, and had made good use of the other facilities offered by the stationer, 'Crest Engraved on Seals or Rings, 7s.; Arms on ditto, 24s.', little thinking that some of his descendants might resent the tax on armorial bearings which became payable as a result whether they were bogus or not, and that others, more inquisitive, might be put to a deal of trouble to discover the authenticity of something he did not for a moment doubt.

In 1835 the retired brewer John Izzard Pryor, living at Clay Hall, Hertfordshire, was assessed by the Surveyor of Taxes for '1 armorial bearing £2. 8s.'. He was a man of his times, a shrewd business man who spent a good proportion of his days working at his accounts in the belief that money was earned by hard work, sober judgement and thrift. Yet he had no ancestral right to those arms, and it was left to his granddaughter, Louisa Mary, three days before her marriage to a cousin of Lord Kilmaine in 1872, to regularise the matter and to obtain a new Grant.

Of course, the use of false arms is not always a hindrance to the genealogist and the arms of a woman quartered by a man's on a book-plate or on a tomb may well give some clue to her surname when this cannot easily be found from other sources. This is made possible by the remarkable book by John Woody Papworth called the *Ordinary of British Armorials* (1874). The heraldic description of a coat of arms proceeds along a certain pattern which enables any coat of arms to be reduced to a written formula which can be understood and turned back into a picture again by any heraldic student. Papworth took all the arms in Burke's *Armory* and other sources and arranged them by their descriptions. Thus a coat of arms can generally be identified through this work. That part of the full achievement of arms which is known as the 'crest' – a word often incorrectly used to describe the whole achievement –

can be identified in the same way from the plates arranged by subject in the second volume of James Fairbairn's *Book of Crests*, the 1905 edition of which must always be used. This book also contains a section identifying mottoes but the most complete list of these is probably still the old *Hand-book of Mottoes* by Charles Elvin (1860). All these books, like Burke's *Armory*, are unofficial, incomplete and often very inaccurate.

Where do we go, then, for official and authentic information? Before discussing that, however, we must go back a little and look at the origins of the subject and the way in which it has developed and been regulated over the centuries.

The medieval knight in full armour made recognition possible by wearing over his mail a surcoat which bore a particular design. That design might be dictated by the shape of the shield on which it was also shown, or by the way in which the latter was made. Because one colour against another colour did not show up at a distance it became a rule that coloured devices or 'charges' could only be placed on 'metal' (i.e. silver or gold) backgrounds, and vice versa. From its use on the knight's surcoat this design was called his 'coat of arms', but it might appear on the knight's banner or lance pennon and on his horse cloth as well.

The oldest arms are certainly the simplest in design and many are no more than a geometric pattern or an exaggeration of the metallic studs and straps used for strengthening the shield, arising almost at whim or by accident. Others took some part of their design from the arms of their feudal lord. The sheaves of wheat in the arms of the Earls of Chester appear in the arms of many Cheshire families such as Cholmondeley and Kevilioc. In Leicestershire the cinquefoil of the Earl of Leicester was similarly used. The latter, A. C. Fox-Davies suggests in *A Complete Guide to Heraldry*, was originally the pimpernel flower used by Robert, Earl of Leicester as a badge in honour of his mother Pernelle or Petronilla, the heiress of Grantmesnil. The family of Staunton of Longbridge who held their land by the service of repairing a tower of Belvoir

Castle derived their arms of two chevrons from those of the Albini lords of Belvoir.

In the fourteenth century there are cases where the owner of a coat granted part of it to someone in his service. The use of these charges does not imply any family relationship, although in other cases it is clear that some families related only by marriage used variations of the same basic coat. In later centuries the granting of similar coats, or coats in which only the tinctures are changed, to persons of the same surname should not necessarily be taken to mean that they were related or believed that they were related but could not prove it.

Many early arms are puns on the names of their owners or on translations thereof, such 'canting' arms appealing to the medieval sense of humour. Thus Martel has hammers in his arms, Trumpington trumpets, Heriz and Maxwell of Herries a hedgehog (herison), Falconer falcons, Corbet crows or ravens, Luttrell an otter (l'outre), Standish three standing dishes, Fishacre a dolphin, Septvans seven winnowing fans, Boller three poppy bolls, Arundell swallows (hirondelle), Comyn garbs or sheaves of cumin, Muschamp flies (musca), Hazlerigg three hazel leaves, Shelley three whelks, Clarke larks, Tempest storm finches, Ratton a rat, Gunter of Tregunter three gauntlets, Fisher a kingfisher, Mauleverer greyhounds (levrier), Rocheid combs, and so on. The varieties are endless, and often the allusions very obscure, but they must have aided identification quite considerably. It is said that the cock in the crest of Law alludes to its cry 'cock-a-leary-law'! In modern grants of arms exactly the same happens, and in 1959 Alan Coxon of Billingham, Durham, was granted two dunghill cocks, and in 1953 Wing-Commander Bulgin received two bull-calves. This practice is certainly to be commended above that by which the modern grantee so often takes something illustrative of his own profession or interests, which may be quite inappropriate to his descendants.

These designs, used by knights on their shields from the first half of the twelfth century to identify each other in battle and at tournaments, were also used as personal symbols to mark their owners' possessions. The lesser knights used the shield of arms alone on their seals. In modern drawings that shield, or 'escutcheon' as it is sometimes called, may be almost any shape according to the whim of the artist. It may, for instance, have a rounded section cut away on the top left-hand side in which to lodge a jousting spear, or the whole may be tilted to one side or '*couché*'. The shape of the shield in drawings is thus no indication of the antiquity of the arms themselves.

By the end of the twelfth century and increasingly in the thirteenth these personal devices, which in battle were the feudal symbols by which fighting men recognised their lord – and with dire consequences if they got them wrong, as when Simon de Montfort relied on the opinion of his barber as to the banners of the approaching army at Evesham in 1265 – were passing from the lord to his descendants, sometimes being altered or 'differenced' (with an additional charge, or by an alteration of the colours or 'tinctures', or by adding a border) according to the relationship, but retaining the main features of the old device. Later, in Tudor times, a regular system of differencing the arms of younger sons in order of birth with special 'cadency' marks was developed, but was used more in theory than in practice.

In addition to the shield, the knight also had a personal 'crest' which he wore on his helmet, like a cock's comb, and which was probably made of dried leather. Such modelled crests did not become common until the fourteenth century. In earlier times the crest may have been a painted design on the helmet itself or on a metal fan fixed to the top of the helmet. The design of the helmet varied according to the rank of the bearer but that of an untitled gentleman came always to be shown as made of steel, with the visor closed and looking towards the left. It is placed in drawings and on seals above the shield, and the crest is shown on the helmet, rising out of the six twists of cloth called the crest wreath which is part of the drapery or 'mantling' which hangs down the back of the helmet to keep the sun off. It is in the arrangement of this mantling, perhaps cut about in battle, that good heraldic artists excel whilst others so often make it appear lifeless or as so much seaweed. It is generally the same colour as the chief colour of the shield and lined with the chief 'metal' – either gold or silver. Sometimes with men of special distinction the crest wreath is replaced by a crest coronet or a chapeau. When all these components were illustrated on large baronial seals, the shield and the helmet, crest, and mantling above were found not to fill the whole available area and so the side spaces were filled with ornamental birds or animals. When drawn and painted on other materials these became in time the 'supporters' which held up the shield. Being associated with the greater barons, the use of such supporters in their arms came in time to be limited to peers and to other very privileged persons.

Supporters date from the early part of the fourteenth century. In modern times examples of their granting to commoners have been the two golden leopards given to George Watson-Taylor, the friend of the Prince Regent, in 1815, and the crocodile and hippopotamus granted posthumously in 1867 to John Hanning Speke, the discoverer of the sources of the Nile.

Supporters stand on a grassy 'compartment' or may 'issue' from a 'watery abiding place', or stand on the motto scroll, the motto used by the family being run on a scroll beneath the shield or over the top of the crest. There are no fixed rules about such matters. This completes the full heraldic 'achievement' or coat of arms, though for most people this will consist of shield, helmet and crest alone.

The motto has very little importance in English heraldry and I always regard mottoes in England as like tartans in Scotland, most being bogus or of very recent origin. The motto is never mentioned in the wording of a 'patent' or grant of arms in England although it may be shown in the margin, and it is not hereditary. It may be assumed and changed at will, but in Scotland it forms part of the Grant of Arms, which will specify how it is to be shown, and it will descend with the arms. The use of mottoes in England did not become general until the eighteenth century, and although some can be traced to a remote period, many of those with which legends are connected were clearly invented centuries after the event commemorated took place.

The crest without the wreath on which it generally stands was later used by itself as a mark of ownership, as on livery buttons, but some great men developed and used personal 'badges' to mark their property and followers. Examples of these are the four-spiked implements called caltraps used by the Drummond family which are said to have been strewn by Sir Malcolm Drummond at the battle of Bannockburn in 1314 to catch in the hooves of the English cavalry, and the belt-buckle used by the Pelham family commemorating the taking of the King of France's belt-buckle by Sir John Pelham after the King's surrender at Poictiers in 1357. The granting of badges was resumed in England in 1905.

The modern pictorial representation of arms owes much to their early use on seals, but already by 1300 they were being used on tombs, first on the recumbent effigy and then as a decoration on the tomb itself. They were soon used on buildings, in stone, wood and glass, and as decorations in manuscripts and on ecclesiastical vestments.

There were, however, surprisingly few arms actually in use, perhaps only fifteen hundred by 1300, a number which possibly doubled in the next 150 years. That the designs adopted, however, did not more often clash is also surprising. The designs seem only rarely – contrary to popular belief – to have been devised as symbolic of some virtue or to commemorate an exploit. The symbolism of the lion and of the eagle is easy to understand, but I doubt whether notions that a black shield represented dignity and sobriety or that gold denoted stainless honour, for instance, ever entered their originators' heads. Stories of exploits like those attributed to the Hay family to account for the arms they used are generally late inventions of no historical value, sad though this is. In the case of the Hays it is said that about 980 the Danes had defeated the Scots at the battle of Luncarty, and that the Scots were stopped in their flight down a narrow defile by an old Scotsman and his two sons carrying plough yokes. They upbraided their countrymen with cowardice, persuaded them to renew the battle and together were victorious. At the end the old man lay wounded on the ground, crying 'Hay, Hay', which word became the family's surname, and for being 'the three shields of Scotland' Kenneth III gave the family a coat of arms showing three small red shields on a white ground, and as much land as a falcon would fly across without settling, which bird the family took as its crest. The story also accounts for the supporters – two countrymen holding ox-yokes – and the motto, 'Serva jugum' ('Preserve the ox-yoke'). Unfortunately it is all nonsense, arms and hereditary surnames at that period being quite unknown, and the name of the family coming much later from a place-name in Normandy. The story was apparently invented, like so many others, by the 'historian' Hector Boece in the early sixteenth century, 'an incorrigible old liar' as Sir James Balfour Paul called him, to account for the arms as they were then used by the Earls of Erroll.

That all these differing coats were assumed without any central control or authority is surprising yet seems to be the case. No one knows how it came about that by the thirteenth century the subject was governed by well defined rules. The knights must have seen each other on expeditions and at tournaments and arranged these things amicably so that similar arms were not used by different families. When disputes arose they were referred to a court presided over by the Constable and the Marshal (subsequently known as the Earl Marshal) which dealt with all military matters. This court is first known to have involved itself with heraldry in 1345. Heralds are known in England from the thirteenth century and the first actual compilation or roll of arms now existing dates from about 1250. However, when the Scrope and Grosvenor trial came before the Court of the Constable and Marshal in 1385 the evidence produced came from charters and the memory of other knights, but not from heralds and rolls of arms. The heralds first appear as organising tournaments, crying the names of the contestants and victors, and only later appear as go-betweens in war. Their ready ability to recognise arms slowly gave them a key position in the development of heraldry. By the middle of the fourteenth century they were recording rolls of arms and a hundred years later it was clearly considered their duty to know and register the arms of noblemen within their areas of jurisdiction – for most heralds had a geographical 'province' within which they alone were allowed to organise tournaments.

In 1415 Henry V instituted the new office of Garter King of Arms in connection with the Knights of the Garter and set him above the other three Kings of Arms, Norroy who had a jurisdiction north of the river Trent, Clarenceux whose jurisdiction was south of the Trent, and March who had a jurisdiction in the West Country and Welsh marches prior to 1500 when these areas were divided between the other two. Very soon after this the Kings of Arms are found making grants of new arms to applicants, but it was only later that their patents of appointment made it clear that they did so on the monarch's authority. The first recorded Grant is that of 1439 to the Drapers' Company of London. There was always a strong feeling, however, that 'arms given by a herald are not of greater authority than those which a man has taken for himself'.

The three Kings of Arms and the other lesser heralds and pursuivants were formed into a corporation in 1484 so that they might have better facilities for the keeping of their records, but disputes between them were not uncommon, many were chosen 'for quite other qualities than skill in genealogy', and they did not have a settled home until their present building in Queen Victoria Street, London, EC4, was completed in the 1680s. The extremely incomplete nature of the records of grants prior to 1673 reflects their many upheavals throughout this period. The turmoil in England, however, was nothing to that in Scotland where in 1569 the chief herald, Sir William Stewart of Luthrie, was burnt 'for conspyring to take the Regent's lyffe by sorcery and necromancy'.

The granting of new arms was given an impetus by Henry VIII's patent to Clarenceux King at Arms in 1530, directing him to grant arms to spiritual persons of suitable degree and to temporal persons who by their services were 'increased or augmented to possessions and riches able to maintain the same', providing the grants were registered in the Earl Marshal's books. The number of their grants grew steadily into Elizabethan times and a property qualification and scale of fees came to be devised. In the 1530s the property qualification was lands or possessions of free tenure to the yearly value of £100 or movable goods worth £360, the fee paid being about £6. It was, as Sir Anthony Wagner said, 'an admirably precise valuation of gentility'. In 1588 gentility was summed up by Serjeant Doderidge in the Abergavenny case as being possessed by those 'who can live idle, and without manuall labour'. Many of these early grants were to guilds and the higher ecclesiastics and to members of the new middle class who were 'able to uphold the honour of nobless', and other grants merely confirmed arms recently assumed or already in use, though that itself might be a euphemism for a new grant.

With the decline in the military use of arms there was a corresponding increase in their use as pure decoration and a fashion for quartering arms grew up, so that the risk of incorrect arms being concocted and used was great. In earlier times the conservation of a woman's arms in those of her husband and children had been achieved by compounding the two coats into one. For a married couple two halves of their shields might be joined in a process called 'dimidiation', but later after the wife died her arms were placed on the second and third quarters of a 'quartered' shield, those of the husband being repeated on the first and fourth quarters. The practice came into general use in England under Edward III, who quartered the arms of England and France on his shield. The woman had to be an heiress for this to happen. During the lifetime of her husband it became general later for her arms to be shown on a central smaller shield called an 'inescutcheon of pretence' and only her children quartered the arms. Later on marriages to other heraldic heiresses may be commemorated in the same way but it is common for only a few of the most important matches to be shown in this way. The use of these quarterings is purely optional. In the sixteenth century it is not common to find more than six or eight quarterings shown, but once the craze started there was of course no reason why it should not be extended indefinitely, and in the eighteenth and nineteenth centuries schemes of a hundred or more are not unknown. In the eighteenth century a scheme containing 892 coats was devised for the Dukes of Northumberland, but the record for officially recorded quarters is said to be that of the family of Lloyd of Stockton in Chirbury, Shropshire, though many of their quarterings are repeated owing to constant intermarriage.

The Court of the Earl Marshal, also known as the Court of Chivalry, continued to deal with disputed cases, the office of Constable ceasing after 1521, but a wider surveillance was needed to deal with the illegal assumption of arms by those not worthy. The heralds had been visiting their provinces in the course of their normal work since the middle of the fifteenth century, but in 1530 the provincial Kings of Arms were empowered 'to reforme all false armorye & Armes devysed without auctoritie' and the regular series of 'Visitation Commissions' of which this was the first, continued every twenty years or so and did not cease until 1686. The patent of 1530 'set up permanent machinery for the exclusive control by the Kings of Arms of all forms of heraldic display within their respective provinces'. They toured the provinces recording the descents of those entitled to arms, taking the names of those described as 'Knight', 'Esquire' and 'Gentleman' from the lists of freeholders liable for jury service and later from the Hearth Tax Returns; and they appointed Deputies in various places to keep an eye on the display of arms at funerals (for which degrees of pomp and scales of fees were fixed), on monuments and on coaches. Together they were given access to records and buildings and powers to deface unauthorised arms. Several false arms on tombs in St Paul's Cathedral and other London churches were defaced in that first year.

At these visitations the heralds or their deputies entered in their books those whose arms were already recorded at the College or had been allowed by a former King of Arms, those who had new grants, and those who could show that their ancestors had used arms for some considerable time, perhaps sixty or eighty years. (At the later visitations respite of a claim for further proof was accepted practice, but if the proof was not forthcoming the provisional entry gave the arms no validity.) Their descents were to be recorded as far back as 'the memory of any man living can reach' and were to be extended further if authentic evidences could be provided. From 1570 onwards those whose pedigrees were entered were required to sign the book. An office copy was usually made later, and perhaps others. Those whose right to arms could not be established had to sign a form of Disclaimer and lists of these were publicised as far as possible locally, forbidding them to be styled 'gentlemen'.

Some visitation pedigrees were clearly compiled at great speed and may lack accuracy on that account, but the great majority of the pedigrees, which are for the most part relatively short and simple, are immensely valuable. However, many copies of them, made for various purposes, have come into private hands and been augmented and 'improved' from both reliable and unreliable sources and it is generally from these that the printed versions have been taken. Many are found in the publications of the Harleian Society taken from copies now in the British Library and their respective values are discussed in *The Visitation Pedigrees and the Genealogist,* by G. D. Squibb (1964).

The exhaustive and periodic nature of the Visitations, the commissions for which were not renewed after the Revolution of 1688, must mean that for large areas of the country the great majority of families claiming to bear arms are included at some time or other. How many escaped the net it is impossible to say but my impression is that the numbers who did were not great. Consequently it is to be regretted that not more of the official pedigrees have been published. There is a list of the dates and areas for which they were made at the back of Sir Anthony Wagner's *The Records and Collections of the College of Arms* (1952) and references to those pedigrees which have been printed will be found in the bibliographies mentioned at the beginning of the second chapter of this book.

The marshalling of arms at funerals had become a prerogative of the Kings of Arms in each province by the fifteenth century, Garter retaining the right in connection with Peers and Knights of the Garter. The fees from this source were considerable. The records of the arms carried at the funeral and the details of the family of the deceased, known as funeral certificates, were returned to the College between 1568 and 1692 and are of great genealogical interest. An index of some which have been printed will be found in *The Genealogist*, New Series, volume 12. The deputies licensed by the College for this work were in many cases merely local arms painters: one, perhaps unique in this field, was a woman, Jane Horsley of York, widow, appointed in 1681. However, in the course of the seventeenth century their monopoly in the painting of arms slowly weakened and in 1692 the House of Lords held that private persons were not punishable by or answerable to proceedings in the Court of Chivalry for assuming to make arms, order funerals without authority, and paint arms contrary to Heraldry. The practice of appointing Deputy Heralds thereafter practically ceased and after 1705 no more were appointed until 1761 when the last, Edward Orme, the organist at Chester Cathedral, was given a jurisdiction in Cheshire and North Wales. He died in 1777.

In spite of the powers given to the heralds in 1530 and the subsequent series of visitations, it seems quite clear that the granting of new arms to the middle class of the Elizabethan period had begun to bring the whole subject into disrepute. In the seventeenth century it seems to have been the common belief that anyone 'could buy a coat of arms for forty shillings' or five marks, as Christopher Billop said 'in scandalous words provocative of a duel' to Christopher Cooper, a lieutenant in Lord Strange's Regiment in 1639, claiming that he 'was a better gentleman'. Actions arising from comments that a person's arms 'came down by the last carrier' and suggestions to a neighbour that he should 'aske Baker when you see him what his armes or gentery cost him' were brought to the Court of Chivalry as 'scandalous words'. It is no wonder that Sir Christopher Yelverton refused to pay fees to the College of Arms for his father's funeral in 1630 and spoke in a deprecating manner of the power and authority of the Earl Marshal and his court, a court which, as another said, gave every opportunity to those 'whose malice hath not end or lymitt', and which could spend many hours discussing whether a gentleman who became a soap boiler thereby lost his gentility.

Such cases were brought within the jurisdiction of the Court by allegations that the plaintiff was no gentleman, and that the words complained of were such as to be likely to provoke him into defending his honour in a duel, duels being regarded as 'deeds of arms', over which the Court had jurisdiction by virtue of a statute of Richard II. In 1634 Nicholas Bestney of St Dunstan in the West, London, said that Thomas Starkey of St Bride's, London, gentleman, 'was a foundling found in a ditch in Lancashire, and a base rascal, and that he was fed on the scraps from Bestney's brothers' and sisters' trenchers' and that he 'had publicly exercised base and machanical arts as a tailor and broker and seller of remnants of cloth', for which Bestney was put in the King's Bench Prison until he produced a bond for good behaviour and paid damages and the costs.

The powers of the Court of Chivalry had been reaffirmed by a Patent of Charles II in 1662 but the decision of 1692 must have been a serious blow to its prestige. It continued down to 1707 to bring cases against persons who wrongly assumed arms and used them on monuments and particularly on coaches, and there was an attempt to revive it between 1731 and 1735, but thereafter until this century it did not sit again.

Heraldry became in the eighteenth century almost entirely the preserve of the engravers and coach-painters and many of the officers of the College of Arms were held in very low repute, their standard declining deplorably. The decline of the heralds' authority gave plenty of scope to vendors of false arms like the notorious Robert Harman, an Irish dancing-master at Ipswich, who made considerable sums therefrom prior to his conviction in 1727. Sir William Blackstone wrote in the 1760s that 'the marshalling of coat-armour had fallen into the hands of certain officers called heralds, who had allowed for lucre such falsity and confusion to creep into their records that even their common seal could no longer be received as evidence in any court of justice'. William Oldys, the author of a well-known *Life of Sir Walter Raleigh* (1736), was got out of a debtor's prison by the Earl Marshal and appointed Norroy King of Arms in 1755. Addicted to low company and rarely sober, he completely disgraced himself at the funeral of Princess Caroline in 1757 and was, as Sir Anthony Wagner has said, 'wholly ignorant of heraldry'. In 1760 he granted to Edward Tetlow of Haughton, Lancashire, what is probably one of the worst heraldic creations known, containing in the crest alone a silver penny on which was written the Lord's prayer, in front of a red book with gold clasps, on which stood a dove holding a black crow-quill pen in its beak!

However, the appointment of heralds like Ralph Bigland in 1757 and Isaac Heard in 1759 eventually brought new standards to the College. The visitations had turned the heralds from ceremonial officers to genealogists. Of course they continued to attend Coronations and the opening of Parliament, to read Proclamations and attend Garter Services, and Garter himself introduces new peers into the House of Lords, but following the visitations their work as genealogists has not ceased to grow and the vast collections of Bigland and Heard amply illustrate this point.

The provision of pedigrees for quite new classes of inquirers is reflected in Bigland's interest in tombstones (as shown in his *History of Gloucestershire*) and in parish registers, a general work on which he published in 1764. The collections of Sir Isaac Heard, Garter from 1784 to 1822, reflect the great growth in the romantic interest in heraldry during that period, the growth of the middle class in that era of the industrial revolution, and the honours showered on commanders both naval and military throughout the Napoleonic Wars. Among his books at the College of Arms is a volume recording the arms of Henry Christophe, the negro Emperor of Haiti, and of his nobility, in 1811.

The publication of records and the standards of proof required in peerage claims in the nineteenth century did much to promote the scientific construction of pedigrees and the fortunes of the College and its standing revived. A succession of very able men in the last century and this has coped with the growing demand for pedigrees and arms, developing new techniques to deal with new problems and exploring new records. Their place in the history of genealogical technique is shown in the present Garter's *English Genealogy.* In this century the Kings of Arms have granted more new arms than in the whole of the previous history of the College. The charges have increased considerably over the years. In 1963 they were a hundred and fifty guineas, but a new scale introduced in 1974 brings them up to a minimum of £400 for private individuals and £650 for corporations. Many grants are to persons living abroad and to Americans, Garter claiming the right to make honorary grants to American citizens of British descent, but I wonder how many today would think the fee 'an admirably precise valuation of gentility' as was said of that in 1530! The officers of arms take it in turns to be in waiting for the reception of visitors and correspondence at the College, Monday to Friday, 10 a.m. to 4 p.m., but the records are not in any way open to public inspection and searches in them may only be accomplished by employing an officer to carry out the work.

There is no official published list of persons to whom Grants of Arms have been made but a very large number, and perhaps most between 1687 and 1898, are indexed in volumes 66–68 of the publications of the Harleian Society. Before 1687 one should perhaps take into account the coverage of the Visitations and the incomplete nature of the records of grants at the College. However, volume 66 of the Harleian Society should be consulted and, for references to the manuscripts in the British Library, the index of Grants and Certificates of Arms compiled by Arthur Jewers and published in volumes 13–29 of the New Series of *The Genealogist* (1897–1913). Many holders of later grants are detailed in the various editions of Fox-Davies's *Amorial Families*, the best of which is that for 1929, but none are anywhere near complete. At the College itself is a most important series of volumes compiled from the early records by Sir Albert William Woods between 1842 and 1904, known as 'Garter's Ordinaries', which enables the heralds to identify any coat of arms brought to them and allows them to make sure that no new coat granted is the same as a previous one.

At the end of the last century it seems to have been generally thought that the Court of the Earl Marshal no longer existed. The *Encyclopaedia Britannica*, for instance, said: 'Its powers fell into disuse, and not long since it was finally abolished, and with it fell any pretence on the part of the college to regulate, by compulsory authority, the heraldry of the kingdom.' However, the writer was mistaken, for in 1954 the Court of Chivalry was revived to hear the complaint of the Corporation of Manchester against Manchester Palace of Varieties Limited that the latter was using its arms on the pelmet above the stage and on its common seal. It was then held that the Court had 'jurisdiction to deal with complaints relating to the usurpation of armorial bearings', but taking into account that 'it is common knowledge that armorial bearings are widely used as a decoration or embellishment without complaint' it was decided that 'use or display in such circumstances would not be a ground for intervention by this Court'. In view of the use of the arms on the common seal, however, the Palace of

Varieties were ordered not to make any further display of the Corporation's arms.

In his judgment Lord Goddard said, 'If therefore it is laid down as a rule of this Court, as I would very respectfully suggest to His Grace the Earl Marshal it should be, that leave must be obtained before any proceedings are instituted, it would I think prevent frivolous actions and if this Court is to sit again it should be convened only where there is really some substantial reason for the exercise of its jurisdiction. Moreover, should there be any indication of a considerable desire to institute proceedings now that this Court has been revived I am firmly of opinion that it should be put upon a statutory basis, defining its jurisdiction and the sanctions it can impose.' That is where the matter rests to this day.

It would thus appear that a man has no redress in England if another person uses his arms, although for a fee any man can have himself made a gentleman, and that a person who is honoured by the crown will not nowadays, because of the fees involved, necessarily obtain the grant of arms which was for so long considered the first degree in nobility or gentility. The great Lord Chancellor, Lord St Leonards, the son of a London hairdresser, who was made a peer in 1852 and died in 1875, seems to have been one of the first peers to refuse a grant of arms, but now it appears a not uncommon practice. When so many grants are being made and there is such a great interest in the subject, this is clearly a most unhappy state of affairs. As a writer in *The Heraldry Gazette* has said, 'Unless the Court of Chivalry is reanimated, heraldry may well deteriorate, and far from being a noble science will be more regarded as an expensive and pointless game.'

The College of Arms has always been financially self-supporting. The fees charged have balanced the cost of maintaining the establishment. This is not the case in Scotland where the Lord Lyon King of Arms and his staff form no corporation or college but are salaried public servants housed in a public building. Their authority derives from Acts of Parliament of 1672 and 1867 but the post of Lord Lyon, which is held direct from the Crown, is of greater antiquity. He is supreme in all matters of heraldry in Scotland and the wrongful assumption of arms there is punishable by fine and imprisonment.

Scottish heraldry differs considerably from that in England and all persons using arms are required to register or 'matriculate' their right in the Lyon Court, the arms of the younger branches being differenced accordingly. The arms of Scottish families living in the Commonwealth may also be registered there. No visitations were made in Scotland and the records of those who have recorded their right to arms and received new grants commence only in 1672. A complete index to them has been published by Sir James Balfour Paul in his *An Ordinary of Arms contained in the Public Register of all Arms and Bearings in Scotland* (1903) and for the background, *Scots Heraldry* (1956) by Sir Thomas Innes of Learney should be consulted. Inquiries should be made to the Lyon Clerk, New Register House, Edinburgh, but the office does not undertake research in the way that the College of Arms does in England and for that a searcher will have to be employed.

The Lyon Office will not normally answer queries about tartans and for information about these the Scottish Tartans Society, Comrie, Perthshire, should be consulted. The museum of the Society has 1300 specimens of tartan, the largest collection in the world.

They seem to show that clans did not have tartans, but that certain patterns were produced in particular areas. The wearing of tartan, except by the Highland Regiments, was forbidden in 1745 and the present 'correct' mode of wearing tartan derives from this military usage. The ban was lifted in 1782, when the traditional patterns were revived. Their use was given an impetus by George IV's visit to Holyrood in 1822, arranged by the romantically-minded Sir Walter Scott, and the majority of modern tartans date from that time.

The correspondence of Wilsons of Bannockburn, perhaps the most important firm of tartan weavers in the eighteenth and nineteenth centuries, is particularly revealing as to the origins of some of the designs. Doreen Field, writing in *Scottish Field* in May, 1977, says: 'Wilsons toured the Highlands to find inspiration for their early patterns, often giving them no more than a number. One pattern had changed from No. 2 to No. 43, then No. 155 or "Caledonia". When a gentleman from Buchan called Kidd continued to buy it in quantity, the pattern metamorphosed into the Kidd tartan in Wilsons' books. When Kidd died, it began to be sold to, and called, MacPherson. In 1822, when George IV visited Scotland on his celebrated tour, carefully stage-managed by Sir Walter Scott who exhorted the clan chiefs to "get their tartans sorted out", the then MacPherson chief, Cluny MacPherson, consulted Wilsons to find his correct wear. He was given the by-then MacPherson tartan which 20 years earlier had been Kidd and a little before that, No. 155'. The story helps to put tartan mania into perspective.

Edward VI appointed the first Ulster King of Arms for Ireland, where the Earl Marshal exercised no jurisdiction, in 1552. He had powers to inspect, determine and correct arms, to impose differences, and to grant new arms by patent. The records of grants exist from that time, and there is a valuable series of funeral certificates from 1588 to 1729 and of registered pedigrees.

Because of the difficulties of proving Irish pedigrees, arms which can be proved to have been used for more than a hundred years may be confirmed by patent.

Since the division of Ireland, the powers of the Ulster King of Arms with regard to Northern Ireland have been transferred to Norroy King of Arms at the College in London, he being styled 'Norroy and Ulster King of Arms'. In the Republic, however, the former office of the Ulster King of Arms in Dublin, together with all the records, has been turned into the Genealogical Office at Dublin Castle with the Chief Herald of Ireland at its head, and his authority is the primary one in Ireland.

Chapter 8

Surnames and Christian Names

In the way that amateur genealogists are so fond of boring each other with accounts of their searches, the professionals bore each other with the unusual names that they have come across in the course of their searches. There are plenty about. Two of the choicest appear in the Introduction to the late Dr P. H. Reaney's *The Origin of English Surnames* (1967), undoubtedly the best book to have appeared on the subject, being the names of gentlemen called Original Bugg and Ephraim Very Ott which he came across in the last war.

Perhaps I will be forgiven if I include two groups of which I am very fond. One was collected from parish registers by Reginald Hine in my native Hertfordshire, and includes Giver Battell, Ghost Butteridge, Paternell Bunne, Lamentation Caudle, Plampin Cooley, Adam Eve, King Fisher, Osbingoldsbey Humblebee, Repentance Peacock, Zilpher Spittle, Lazarus Stops, Greediana Tarboy, Tobias Trim, Adored Tuffnail, Wigmore Wiskin and Battalion Shotbolt. The other I found when helping to put in order the half-million index slips to testators in the Prerogative Court of Canterbury between 1750 and 1800. From letters 'I' and 'J' I culled Originall Ims, Bloomer Ireland, Emblen Ivye, Tom Jupiter, Emerjentiana Jenkinson and Slodden Jelly, but in letter 'S' I rejoiced with Fleet Scurry, Carnaby Scarff, Sex Sedula, John Skunk, Francis Skull, Christian Skinn, Striker Slater, Dirk Slinger, The Hon. Wigbold Slicher, Christopher Sloggett, Climacteric Smith, North South, Carnaby Strutt, Agatha Six, Frostan Snow, The Lady Cornelia Splinter, and the Revd Angel

Silke, and (mis-filed) September Black.

As I have said, many start their genealogical searches because of the rareness of their surname, wondering from what area of the country it derives, and, perhaps, what it means. The origin of surnames is a subject fraught with difficulty on which much has been published, but there is not a single work that has not been castigated as 'useful but dangerous' by modern scholars. The amateur who looks up his surname in one of the many dictionaries of surnames – the best known being C. W. Bardsley's *A Dictionary of English and Welsh Surnames* (1901) and P. H. Reaney's *A Dictionary of British Surnames* (1961) – will very rarely be finding anything that relates to his actual surname and in many cases he must go unsatisfied. Names have altered so much over the years in so many families that unless the ancestry is traced back in the male line to the first bearers of the name, and the earliest possible forms of the name found, then all other research is so much idle speculation quite irrelevant to any particular family. Thus a person with the name Bruce may descend from the Norman family of Briouze, lords of Bramber in Sussex in 1086, or it may go back to a King of Scotland, but on the other hand it may, more than likely, derive from the worker in a brew-house. In the same way, how does a person called Pick or Pyke or Peake know whether he is descended from a pikeman, a man who is as thin as a pike, who acts like a woodpecker, who sells pike, who makes peck measures, or who lives by the peak or by Pick Hill, unless he traces something of the early history of his family, and even then he may well not be able to come to any conclusions.

As Dr Reaney said, 'The man who says his name was always spelled as it is today is talking rank nonsense.' Present day forms of a large number of our surnames are due to the spelling of some sixteenth- or seventeenth-century parson, or even to a registrar of births in the nineteenth century, who had no guide to the spelling of names. Indeed, no recognised system of spelling existed, and any idea that one spelling was more 'correct' than any other hardly entered their heads. The great majority of the population were illiterate, they gave their names orally and the clerk put them into writing as best he could, perhaps using a different spelling at different times. The problem is understood by most people when reading old writings, as when that curious Welshman 'affer david' turns out to be an 'affidavit', but many are quite unwilling to accept it when it applies to their own surnames. Tristram Farrer appears in the parish registers of Rothwell in Yorkshire as both Farrey and Farrah, probably deriving from the Old French *ferreor,* meaning 'smith', a surname which also develops as Farrow and Faro, and is found in Suffolk as Pharrow in the seventeenth century and as Pharaoh in the eighteenth, where it still survives, and where many would give an Egyptian origin to it.

Changes of this kind account for many curious modern names which are thought by their bearers to be foreign and which are not found in older records, and it is only by genealogical research that their true origins are discovered. Thus the present Goulby is found to come from Goulsbra, Ivereigh from Ivory, and Kellett is found earlier as Qualet, a name which itself is probably a variant of something else. The name Iles is pronounced and found as Oils and Eyles in some parts of the country, but Hoyle is a south Yorkshire pronunciation of Hole.

There is a marked tendency in dialect to add an 's' to words beginning with a consonant and thus names arise lkie Scripps from Cripps, and Sturgess from Turgoose, but in reverse Stacey becomes Tacey, and Trafford comes from the place Stretford in Lancashire. The 'S' may become an initial 'Sh' as in Shakesby from the place-name Saxby; it is not a variant of Shakespeare. Loss of an 'r' is common, as in names like Basham and Bassam from places called Barsham, and Antcliff from Arncliffe in Yorkshire. The initials 'P' and 'B' interchange, as in Peasegood and Bisgood from Peascod, and Boumphrey and Pumfrey from ab or ap Humphrey. Similarly with 'T' and 'D', with Tennyson probably a variant of Dennison, Tyson of Dyson, and Tandy of Dandy. The final 'n' in 'son' may change to an 'm', as in Ransom and Cursham for Curzon. The unstable 'h' produces Heavens from Evans, Hartwright from Arkwright, and Hexter from Exeter. The pronunciation of 'F' as 'V' produces Venner from Fenner, Vowles from Fowle and Fidler from Vidler. Many more examples of this kind may be found in Reaney's book and they should be studied with great care by those who have lost the track of their ancestors and think that they may be lurking locally in some variant spelling as yet unrecognised.

All our original ancestors had a single name, whether Celts, Anglo-Saxons, Normans or Scandinavians. Certain people before the Conquest and in growing numbers afterwards had an additional 'byname', but these names were not in any way hereditary surnames in the modern sense. Thus Eadulf Campa is found in Wiltshire in 902, and Aluric Camp was dispossessed of his lands in Essex, Cambridgeshire and Suffolk by William the Conqueror, but these descriptive names, from the Old English *cempa* meaning 'a warrior' would not have passed to their sons or descendants, and it seems likely that the modern Camps derive their surname from the place-name Castle Camps in Cambridgeshire.

By the twelfth century there is an unsettled and varied usage of names which is often descriptive: thus people were known by their single baptismal names, or by this followed by their father's name in full or his baptismal name, or by this followed by the name of their estate or place of origin, or by a byname descriptive of their office or occupation or which is a nickname. In different documents they may appear in different combinations of these names. Thus Adinet de Bidyk appears in the Essex Assize Rolls in that name and also as Adnettus le Taylur. 'Ralph de Eyr called Proudfot of Havering' appears in the Hornchurch Priory documents in the same county a century later. Henry Lordessonne alias Henry de la Heus appears in a Northamptonshire charter of 1460. Roger Harflete otherwise Roger Checker son and one of the heirs of Christopher Harflete otherwise called Christopher Atcheker appears in Kent in 1508, and shows how this general instability may continue into a period long after most hereditary surnames have become fixed. Some of these aliases continue in families for at least a further two hundred years, and it is a phenomenon I have noticed particularly in Somerset. The late Erik Chitty was able to discover the origin of an interesting one when in 1371 Richard Toly gave over to Thomas Cheteye and his heirs a house and piece of land which had once belonged to John Cokkel. In 1453 he found Thomas Chetty of Cokkelys named in the Hundred Rolls, and in 1558 he found the will of one John Chetty alias Coklys.

Some of these early variations of names as they are found in documents are merely scribal translations of one name. Thus in Domesday Book one Robert *blundus* is also called *albus, flavus* and *blancard*, all meaning 'the fair', and the tenants of Woolfin in Devonshire had their names translated into Latin and French by different scribes at different periods and appear as Gregory Lupus, Richard le Low and Walter Wolf. The surnames as given in the documents, however, may differ from those used by the men themselves, as sometimes appears from their names on the seals.

Some variations in names may also result from apprenticeship, for it seems to have been quite common, at least in London in the thirteenth and fourteenth centuries, for apprentices to take their master's surnames. A very good example of this is Thomas de Cavendishe, son of William atte Watre de Ewelle, who was admitted to the freedom of the city in 1312, and had been the apprentice of Walter de Cavendishe, mercer, although his original surname would presumably have been atte Watre or de Ewelle. Thus not all Cavendishes come from the place of that name in Suffolk.

In the last century it seems to have been the quite common belief that all persons of the same surname must be related and such traditions die hard. Even A. L. Rowse in his *A Cornish Childhood* when speaking of his maternal cousins named Courtenay, a mining family which had gone to South Africa and then on to America, says, 'There is no doubt that they would go back to the original stock of the Courtenays, Earls of Devon', but how can he be sure of this when the adoption of a master's surname by an apprentice or servant seems not to have been uncommon?

Surnames may be divided into four main groups: local surnames, surnames of relationship, surnames of occupation or office, and nicknames.

By far the greatest number derive from place-names and indicate where a man held land, or the place from which he had come or where he actually lived. They derive from places in England, Scotland and in France, and although before the Conquest they were generally preceded by the preposition 'at', 'on' or 'in', after the Conquest it was generally 'de' whether the place-name was English or French. The French name might be the seat of a noble family, but it might as easily be the place from which an ordinary French family had migrated. Very occasionally the name may come from an inn sign, like atte Lamb or atte Raven, but some of these supposed 'signs' may in fact be topographical landmarks, such as Ball or Cock. Many modern surnames derived from places are misleading and do not indicate such an origin. Thus Slaughter may have been a butcher, but he may also have come from Upper or Lower Slaughter in Gloucestershire. Thicknesse comes from a place of that name in Staffordshire, Trickey from the place in Devonshire. Raspberry from Ratsbury in Devon and Courage from Cowridge in Luton are other good examples.

Professor Black in his valuable *The Surnames of Scotland* (1963) says that Trollope may be of local origin as suggested by Lower, 'although the place from which it was assumed has been forgotten', but Reaney has found it to be Troughburn in Northumberland, formerly called Trolhop and meaning 'troll-valley'. The surname Brighton comes from the place of that name in the East Riding of Yorkshire (now Breighton), for the spelling Brighton for the place in Sussex is a modern corruption of Brightelmeston or Brighthelmstone. Similarly Bristol is from the places Burstall and Birstal in Yorkshire, the great West Country port being in the middle ages called Bristow, from Brycgstow 'the place by the bridge', giving rise to the surnames Bristow and Brister (though some at least of these may derive from Burstow in Surrey).

Large numbers of English local surnames derive from small places and denote residence by a wood, etc., for example, atte wode, atte fenne, and atten oke, and become Attlee, Byfield, Uphill and Underdown, etc. The prepositions before all these names tended to die out between 1300 and 1400, the process being much more rapid in the south than in the north.

Surnames deriving from relationships are often called patronymics, but sometimes come from the mother and not from the father, as well as from other relationships, for *-magh* means 'brother in law', as in Watmough. Johnson and Williamson are obvious examples of surnames derived from a father, but Mawson and Moulson come from the mother, Matilda, as do Tilson and Tillotson from its pet-name, Tillie. Similarly Penn may come from Parnell (from Petronilla) and Honeyball from Anabel (from Mabel). The occurrence of names of this sort has been used to throw light on the usage of Christian names generally, and of the changes from English to Norman names, but it is a subject that has many pitfalls. The Old English names seem to have survived longer in the provinces than in the capital, but as early as about 1100 English people were giving their children French names, and thus it is quite clear that a French name does not mean a French descent. After 1200 the old English Christian names are hardly found in London, although a few names from the old royal family and the saints survived.

Surnames derived from occupations and offices are frequent, but many were clumsy and have disappeared. Steward, Chancellor, Constable, Reeve, Sergeant, from offices, and Ashburner, Tanner, Farmer, Cheesewright, Lister (dyer), Barker (tanner) and Harbisher (maker of hauberks) are examples. There is a surprising variety, and Fransson has noted a hundred and sixty-five different surnames deriving from occupations in the cloth industry alone. Names like Kitchener and

Buttery must be occupational, but Prior, Abbot, Monk and Nun are presumably nicknames since, of course, such people were presumably celibate. The latter category of names may describe physical attributes or peculiarities, as with Head, Redhead, Sheepshanks, Garnham ('moustache') and Grelley ('pock-marked'); or mental and moral characteristics, like Sharp, Wise, Pennyfather ('miser') and Gulliver ('glutton'); or dress and equipment, as with Hood and Shorthouse; or they may be nicknames derived from oaths used, such as Godsave, or derogatory occupational names, such as Fettiplace (usher), Catchpole (constable) and Knatchbull (butcher). The varieties are legion and one can well understand the attraction of studies of this kind.

Although the new French personal names which were coming into England after the Conquest were more varied than has been commonly believed it seems likely that surnames came into being to a large extent as a means of differentiating between the numerous individuals with the same Christian name. The growth of feudalism required the exact identification of more and more people. At first the upper classes, with whom the feudal officials were chiefly concerned, assumed and were given names, and the process spread to the lower classes. They began to pass from father to son, to become hereditary, amongst the noblemen in the early twelfth century, but among the ordinary people they did not come into general use until the next century, although by the end of it they were fairly frequent. The custom increased rapidly in the fourteenth century and by 1500 most people in England had hereditary surnames. Material to show when a name passed from father to son is unfortunately in most cases lacking, although one can easily see in early documents that when a man is following an occupation different to that of his occupational surname then the surname is probably hereditary. Again, where the surname is derived from an Old English personal name which is no longer in use in the area, one must assume that it has been inherited from an earlier time. All these processes seem to have followed much later in the north than they did in the south, and it is there that names ending in *-son* began to be assumed about 1380.

These remarks relate to England. In Wales hereditary surnames are a post-sixteenth century development, and they are for the greater part patronymics. It was a very slow process and in the nineteenth century was still not complete, some people in Merionethshire still taking their fathers' Christian names as their surnames. In this century the need for differentiation has caused many to take additional surnames, such as Addams-Williams or Astley-Jones.

In Scotland also hereditary surnames were late in developing, particularly in the Highlands, and the clan system resulted in large numbers of people with the same name, but many names are undocumented before the fifteenth or sixteenth centuries, and etymological work is much more difficult. I have mentioned the superb book by Professor Black which, in spite of the difficulties, throws much light on them.

In Ireland patronymics formed by prefixing *O* or *Ua* to the grandfather's name or *Mac* to the father's appear in the middle of the tenth century, but the development of hereditary surnames was slow and spread over several centuries. One result of the Anglo-Norman settlement was that names acquired two forms, one Irish, one English. Some English settlers adopted Irish names, but there were specific attempts made to stamp them out and the anglicisation of Irish names increased after the 1688 revolution. *O* and *Mac* were frequently dropped and names were translated, altered to better-known names, and generally assimilated, making, when further corruptions took place after emigration to England or America, endless difficulties for the genealogist. The works by Edward MacLysaght on Irish surnames, particularly his *A Guide to Irish Surnames* (1967), are the most valuable, but a useful *Varieties and Synonyms of Surnames and Christian Names in Ireland* was published by the Registrar General in Dublin in 1890.

In Northern Ireland a project undertaken by the Ulster Folk and Transport Museum in 1966 to index all the surnames in the electoral lists for the eleven northern counties, from which surname lists for each county are being prepared, will give a most useful indication of the distribution of any surname there.

No similar work has been done in England, and the only attempt to record relative distributions of names here is that by Dr H. B. Guppy in *The Homes of Family Names* (1890) which was based on the names of farmers in Kelly's Post Office Directories and ignored those with a relative frequency of less than seven per ten thousand in a county. However, a survey of English surnames is being carried on by a Research Fellow in the Department of English Local History at Leicester University, the support of the Marc Fitch Fund enabling it to continue. The main object of that survey is to investigate the history of English surnames, with special reference to the distribution and dispersal of surnames, and the distinctive characteristics of the surnames in particular regions. Two volumes on the surnames of the West Riding of Yorkshire and on Norfolk and Suffolk surnames in the Middle Ages have been published as a result of the work of the survey, edited by George Redmonds and R. A. McKinley.

The formation of the Survey of English Surnames group at Leicester University was announced by Sir Anthony Wagner in his Jubilee Lecture to the Society of Genealogists in 1961, 'Genealogy and the Common Man'. The Survey is based to a large extent on the analysis of successive records, beginning with the Subsidy returns and the Poll Taxes.

Many genealogists, not skilled to the extent needed by such a survey, have done valuable work with the study of single surnames and their distribution from more modern records. The techniques were described and discussed by Francis Leeson in in *The Genealogists' Magazine* (1964) and they are being increasingly applied by the members of the One-Name Societies which I shall mention later. Where the surname is sufficiently rare as to allow one to collect all the references to it, the results can be particularly interesting. Doing it myself with the name Norweb(b), which according to Professor Weekley in *Surnames* (1917) was a compound of Webb meaning 'a weaver who lived at the north end of town', I find that every person of this name now living descends from one Thomas Norweb who first appears in history at Wetherby in Yorkshire in 1766 and died at Wrawby in Lincolnshire in 1809. The most extensive searches have not produced any references to the name before that date. But in the last century there was a wealthy sugar refiner called John Browne living at Rotterdam who wrote books on the opera under the pseudonym of J. Norweb, Browne being an anagram of Norweb. Am I then to assume that my first Thomas Norweb, a watchmaker, was also called Browne? And what value can one attach to Professor Weekley's book in such circumstances?

As regards changes of name, the law is and always has been in England, that anybody may change his or her name without any formality whatsoever. The change is effected by merely assuming the new name, but it may be advisable to possess some proof that one has assumed the new name. This is generally provided by deed-poll or by Royal Licence, and occasionally has been done by private Act of Parliament, but in all these cases the name has been changed by voluntary assumption and not by these documents, which are only evidence of the assumption. As long ago as 1730 the Master of the Rolls said, 'I am satisfied that anyone may take upon him what surname and as many surnames as he pleases.' Thus, unfortunately, the great majority of changes of name must have gone unrecorded. If some record has been made or the fact advertised, then some reference may be found in Phillimore and Fry's *An Index of Changes of Name* 1760–1901 (1968). The first instance of a Royal Licence for change of surname is said to be in 1679, when Henry Cavendish was granted permission to take the name of Percy on marrying the heiress of that family.

Many foreigners, as we have seen, have changed their names when coming into this country or during the wars, and it is interesting that shortly before the First World War, Alfred Germany, a journalist at Hendon, London, whose family seems to derive from the Norfolk Jermys, changed his name to

Valdar, and in 1939 Dr George Reginald Germany of Newbold in Derbyshire changed his name to Granton. The composer Sir Edward German, however, had changed his name from Jones.

Fortunately, many who have changed their names appear in documents with aliases which link the various parts of their lives together. Judith Treleven had long been married to her first husband John Sanders, but only for fourteen months to her second husband Sylvester Treleven, and so described herself as Judith Treleven alias Sanders when she made her will in 1696. A child whose father dies early may take the surname of his stepfather, and later couple it with an alias to make the position clear. At Elland in Yorkshire, Henry the illegitimate son of Thomas Hanson and Susanna Flather was baptised in 1619. When his own child Sarah was baptised there in 1658 he was called Henry Hanson alias Flather, and he was buried as Henry Flather alias Hanson in 1677. James Rolfe was the illegitimate son of Elizabeth Rolfe and was baptised at Tidcombe in Wiltshire in 1795. He married as a Rolfe and had his first children baptised in that name, but at the baptism of others called himself Rolfe alias Stroud and finally just Stroud, which was presumably the name of his father. In the later Census Returns he appears just as Rolfe again. Some aliases were adopted for reasons of pride or remembrance, as when apprentices took their masters' names, or when Oliver Cromwell's ancestor Richard Williams changed his name to Cromwell on marriage to the sister of the Earl of Essex. In Scotland many aliases result from a woman's use of her maiden surname in addition to her husband's surname.

It has often been said that baptismal names cannot be changed but it is clear that they frequently are and more often than not a change has been made when a child has been adopted. The best book on Christian names is certainly the *Oxford Dictionary of English Christian Names* by E. G. Withycombe (1950) and she summarises the position by saying, 'it is now usually assumed that a man's legal appellation is the Christian name given him in baptism by his god-parents (or, alternatively, inserted in the registration of his birth) and the surname of his father or, in the case of an illegitimate child, of his mother'.

Christian names are sometimes useful in themselves to genealogists. In England the eldest son may well be named after the father, but further than that one cannot go. In the west of Scotland, however, there existed a highly developed naming pattern. The eldest son was named after the paternal grandfather, the second after the maternal grandfather and the third after the father. The eldest daughter was named after the maternal grandmother, the second after the paternal grandmother, and the third after the mother. In the West of Ireland the eldest son and daughter were named after the father and mother and then the remainder in the same order as in Scotland. Both these are reminiscent of the Jewish naming customs, except that amongst the Ashkenazi Jews children are rarely given the names of living ancestors.

Even where in England there is no logical system the descent of Christian names can be of value, some families having used certain names for many centuries. Where these pass through female lines they can be particularly helpful. Checking for an Alured Lonsdale in the Army Lists I noticed an Alured Faunce in the same Regiment and by looking at printed pedigrees of the latter's family easily found that he was a maternal uncle of the former. The name Theodosia has passed into forty-five different families descended from Sir James Harington of Exton since he so named his eighth daughter. Mildred, the second wife of Lord Burghleigh, gave her name as godmother to the sister of Francis Windebanke, Secretary of State to Charles I. Her granddaughter Mildred Reade married Colonel Augustine Warner, whose younger daughter Mildred married Laurence Washington of Sulgrave. The elder daughter married John Smith of Purton and was the mother of Mildred Smith who married Robert Porteus of Newbottle, Virginia. Their granddaughter Mildred Porteus married Robert Hodgeson of Congleton, Cheshire, and their granddaughter Henrietta Mildred Hodgeson married Oswald Smith of Blendon Hall, Kent. The latter's daughter married the thirteenth Earl of Strathmore, the ancestor of the Queen Mother and of her cousin Mildred Bowes-Lyon.

It would be rash to assume that all families using the name Mildred and living on the estates of this family were related in some manner, however, and the name would pass to other families through sponsorship at baptism. In Scotland there was some custom for the first child to be baptised by a minister in his new parish to be given the minister's name. Other names, well known in one family, have been assumed by unrelated families to cause problems for later genealogists. Thus not all Francis Drakes are related to the Admiral, all Ashley Coopers to the Earl of Shaftesbury, or all Abel Smiths to the Nottingham banker.

Double Christian names in this country are very rare before the later seventeenth century, although isolated examples are found from the fifteenth century. Long before they developed, surnames, often from mothers, were being used as Christian names. Normally this implies kinship, but some names arise from tenancy, as Poyntz was used by sixteenth-century Gloucestershire families. This does not imply an illegitimate descent from the lord of the manor, although when a surname is given as a second Christian name to an illegitimate child it may generally be presumed to be the surname of the father. 'Lucy Bourman, singlewoman', had an illegitimate child called Samuel Button Bourman baptised at Stone-in-Oxney in Kent in February, 1844, and she married the father, Samuel Button of 'Canardington', there in December that year.

The use of surnames as Christian names can be an extremely useful clue to probable ancestry, particularly because of the marriage indexes available it is sometimes easier to find a marriage than it is a baptism. Bilton Warner, a farm labourer at Walkern at the end of the last century was the nephew of another of that name who was the grandson of Henry Warner and Elizabeth Bilton who married at Walkern in 1756, a descent which might have been guessed on finding the latter marriage in Boyd's Marriage Index at the Society of Genealogists.

Chapter 9

Wider Values

'We are having a trawler built', the letter began. It was 1958 and my correspondent wanted to name it after Sir Thomas Masterman Hardy, Nelson's friend, and to invite his descendants, if there were any, to the launching party. In a similar manner the Greek Embassy later conceived the idea of taking to Greece to participate in the one hundred and fiftieth anniversary festivities there the English descendants, if they could be traced, of those who had fought in Greece for that country's independence. Countless airlines and ships wanted to inaugurate new routes started in the bicentenary year of Captain Cook's discoveries by taking his descendants on free trips. Sadly for them, there are none. The builders of a vast new dam and hydro-electricity works in Japan have decorated it with statues of persons famous in the development of electricity. Descendants of these too, if they can be traced, will be taken to Japan and feasted at the opening ceremony.

Again and again such questions arise and it is the genealogist who is asked to provide the answers. No great importance attaches itself to the examples given above, but think how the interest in and value of a chart-case reputed to have gone round the world with Captain Cook and now on loan with a certain museum will increase if the family in which it has come down can be shown to be related to him, as they claim, or again how such searches can acquire value if the descendants are found to possess portraits or papers of the ancestor which were not formerly known to exist.

In the realms of biography such searches are commonplace. It is years since Oliver Wendell Holmes said, 'We are all omnibuses in which our ancestors ride, and every now and then one of them sticks his head out and embarrasses us,' and nothing gives the biographer greater joy than to be able to point to some particular passenger or group of passengers to explain some trait in his subject's character or his physical appearance. Examples are not necessary, but searches of this kind, where some famous person is the subject, can obviously be some of the most interesting from the genealogist's point of view. Now that the lives of so many minor luminaries of the eighteenth and nineteenth centuries are being written, particularly as theses by university students, there is a considerable trade in the tracing of the descendants of these people in the hope, quite often realised, that useful material may be found in their possession, or that further light will be thrown on the background and family relationships of the person in question. The method is generally to look for the will of that person and then for the wills of the persons mentioned in that will, and so on down to the present time, all the while with the desperate hope that the line does not die out or disappear abroad, and that the descendant when found will co-operate with the inquiries being made.

Genealogy has often been called the handmaid of history, and it is in the realms of local history that this is most clearly seen. The sources which the genealogist uses, explores and seeks to preserve, are very often those used most by the local historian. Parish Registers, wills, manor court rolls and census returns are obvious examples. In many cases the genealogist's use of these records came before that of the local historian, as when genealogists early in this century were using Census Returns to unravel problems in the last century, but their value as a source for nineteenth-century local history has only been recognised in the last few years. It has been the genealogist's use of wills that has provided most of the calendars and printed indexes which exist. The British Record Society which has done so much to publish indexes of this kind has always been run by genealogists, and chief among them, its founder, W. P. W. Phillimore, was the first to put forward the idea of County Record Offices in a letter to *The Times* in 1889. By its very existence the British Record Society 'spurred the Public Record Office into the publication of great series of calendars, lists and indexes, and nearly half a century later had been instrumental in setting up an organisation, the British Records Association, for the sorting and distribution of records for preservation.' In the records preservation field it had itself in 1929 sorted no less than thirty thousand documents and sent them to repositories in twenty-eight counties, a work which, through the Association, was particularly important during and after the Second World War.

The historian Dr Peter Spufford in commenting on the value of genealogy to the historian in general has said:

> For the historian it is of little interest to know if some great family of the eleventh century has descendants today – his interest is limited to the period in which the family was of importance and exercised a considerable influence upon the political scene. His interest in the ancestors of public figures is limited to those close ancestors who had a personal impact upon them, and from whom they may have inherited their ability, or to those ancestors who contributed materially to the estates upon which their political power may have been based or to those alliances which built up the kinship group within which they operated. The descent of present day Giffards from Osbern de Bolebec and Wevie the sister-in-law of Richard I Duke of Normandy in the tenth century may in itself be a fascinating piece of information – but it can have no relevance to a study of the close familial relationship between William the Conqueror and those leading barons to whom he enfeoffed so much of England. A long descent can only be of interest to the historian when it is accompanied by continuous possession of property, office or title and a continuous participation in the active life of the nation.

He goes on to suggest where the genealogist can throw light on such national matters: on the build-up of estates and kinship groups amongst the over-mighty subjects who characterised the period of bastard feudalism; on the problems of the rise of the gentry; on intermarriage and the cohesive or fissiparous nature of village society; on the place of family in personal alignments during the Civil War (remembering that kinship implies feeling perhaps of friendship but possibly of aversion); on the importance of family alliances in English politics in the eighteenth century; and on hereditary ability in civil service and academic dynasties.

By way of example he says:

> It is of no relevance to a study of Athelstan who was king from 924 to 940 to know that his great-great-grandfather was called Oslac (a piece of information which a genealogist might cherish), but extremely relevant to know that his sisters were married to the German Emperor Otto the Great, to Charles the Simple, king of France, to Louis II, king of Provence and to Hugh Capet, count of Paris, whilst his aunt was married to Baldwin, count of Flanders. At once the historian is vividly presented with the fact that Anglo-Saxon England in the tenth century was not a backwater, an island to be studied in isolation, but was fully involved in the comity of Europe.

With a pedigree he illustrates the close familial relationship between William the Conqueror and those leading barons to whom he enfeoffed so much of England, and seen in that light the Norman Conquest appears very much a family affair which largely explains why William was able to build up in England a much more orderly and centralised form of feudal society than that existing on the continent. A selective genealogy of the house of York significantly demonstrates the build-up of the land complex which provided the financial resources for the seizure of the throne by Edward IV. Similarly, a pedigree of the family of Sir Edward Seymour shows that of his 'party' of twenty-six members all sitting for West Country seats in the

bones when the tomb was opened in 1874, but recent research has thrown doubt on both pieces of evidence. His body was identified on the battle field not by his fingers, let alone by the arms he carried, but by, of all things, his teeth. It is possible that he suffered from symphalangism but the first person in the family tree for whom there is firm evidence of it is Charles, 2nd Earl Talbot, who died in 1849, and the condition is present in the descendants of three of his seven married sons, and has affected female equally with male members of the family. In addition to the finger abnormality the short bones of the foot and ankle, the tarsal bones, are similarly fused. It has been suggested that an American family descended from a Scottish emigrant named William Brown, in which symphalangism has also been described, could share common ancestry with the Talbots. Francis Leeson, a professional genealogist, has used a condition called brachydactyly, or short digits, in attempts to link two families called Ford which possessed it in Staffordshire and Warwickshire.

Another example which has received much publicity is porphyria variegata, recently labelled the 'Royal Malady', a rare condition inherited as a dominant, which renders those inheriting it liable to abdominal and mental symptoms, skin troubles, and odd paralyses. The 'madness' of George III, who was previously generally assumed to have been a manic depressive, was ascribed to porphyria by Doctors MacAlpine and Hunter in 1968. On previously overlooked evidence, they suggested that both George III and James I suffered from porphyria and that the characters of many of their relations, such as Mary Queen of Scots and Frederick the Great, suggested that they probably suffered from it as well. However, Professor Cochrane has said that because of the wide range of symptoms produced by porphyria it is not difficult to argue a case for its diagnosis in many historical characters, and that the only way to test the hypothesis is by the examination of living descendants of George III, in the hope of establishing the fact of a higher prevalence of porphyria among his descendants than among the general population. Of course, the rare blood disease haemophilia is to be found in the descendants in the female line from Queen Victoria, and it has been suggested to me that it would be unusual for both rare conditions to be found in the same family. An alternative, less satisfactory, approach is to see how many of the known porphyric families can be traced back to the Hanoverians or Stuarts, but Professor Cochrane's work on one such family, which has been traced back to 1100 in one branch and 1500 in another, has revealed no trace of royal blood.

A particularly distressing inherited disease which affects both sexes is Huntington's chorea, in which the victims suffer both physically and mentally from increasing uncoordination. Their children have a fifty per cent chance of developing the disease, and those who do will pass on the same chance to their children. Some generations may appear to skip the disease because the transmitter dies before it develops, but his or her children still have a fifty per cent chance of developing it themselves. All this has been proved by ample genealogical research, and by tracing cousins who may be at risk, doctors working from Dereham Hospital, Norfolk, have been able to help with genetic counselling and specialist advice. Research into this terrible disease has been greatly assisted by the Association to Combat Huntington's Chorea.

Unfortunately for most of us it is not possible to trace the physical characteristics of our ancestors beyond human memory unless portraits survive or successive generations have been in the army or navy and appear in their description books. I always view with the greatest suspicion evidence of relationship based solely on presumed physical appearance, for anyone with experience in this field knows how family likenesses are seen in the most unlikely faces. Numerous Canadians claim to be descended from Queen Victoria's father, the Duke of Kent, through his liaison with Madame de St Laurent, and have deduced in support of their claims amazing likenesses to some member of the royal family, often, as Mollie Gillen in her life of the couple, *The Prince and his lady*, has said, 'with no resemblance stronger than the wearing of a beard or a widow's cap'. Every one of the claims she shattered.

With good portraits, however, I do not deny that one can trace facial characteristics, for as Forst de Battaglia has pointed out, the Queen undoubtedly inherited hers from a French lady, Hyacinthe Gabrielle Roland, who married the Marquess Wellesley in 1794. Their daughter, Anne Wellesley, married Lord William Cavendish-Bentinck whose granddaughter, Nina Cecilia, married the 14th Earl of Strathmore and was the mother of Queen Elizabeth the Queen Mother. The father of Mademoiselle Roland is still not altogether proven but I would not care to judge any applicant by his face alone.

Any genealogist can begin to put accepted theories to the test, however, by tracing the occurrence of twins in his family, as did Mark Hughes in the Goodwin family in Norwich, an account of which he published in *The Genealogist's Magazine* in 1970. An interesting table published by Forst de Battaglia in 1949 shows twenty pairs of twins among the descendants of George II, Landgrave of Hesse-Darmstadt, including one pair among the children of the Count of Paris.

I am often asked for advice by people who want to marry their cousins and are worried about the children of such a marriage. These I usually send in the direction of a doctor. However, the parents of the first Lord Rothschild, who was clearly no fool, were double first cousins and he only had four great-grandparents instead of eight. Joseph, in the Bible, a man of very fine character and ability, was particularly inbred, being by a series of cross-marriages great-great-grandson, great-great-great-grandson, and great-great-great-great-grandson, each twice over, of the same person, and thus had perhaps only eighteen instead of thirty-two great-great-great-grandparents. Inbreeding results not only from social and political forces but also where families exist in small geographically isolated communities. At Damariscotta, Maine, one Arthur Averill Chapman died in 1953 at the age of ninety-six. His paternal grandparents were first cousins, and his maternal grandparents were double first cousins, but there was, as he said, 'not a fool or a horse thief among them'.

Lawyers generally make good genealogists. They know when a relationship is proven and when it isn't. William Brigg certainly neglected his clients and devoted most of his career to copying Parish Registers. I am told that J. B. Whitmore, the compiler of *A Genealogical Guide,* was such another. Some have much opportunity for practising their skills in the intestacy cases which come their way, and professional genealogists have found this kind of work, if they can get it from solicitors and trustee departments, particularly remunerative. As Reginald Hine said, 'It is foolish of people to die intestate. It gives so much more trouble.'

Ida Wood was the widow of the proprietor of the New York *Daily News* whose brother Fernando Wood had been Mayor of New York. In 1907, with her sister and her daughter she moved into the Herald Square Hotel and retired to her room. She did not come out again until 1932 and when she died the following year at the age of ninety-four, 1,103 persons came forward to contend that they were her nearest relatives and to claim the very considerable estate of 'The Recluse of Herald Square'. Intense genealogical activity resulted, with searches in America and Europe until the estate was settled in 1939. The claimants were characterised by Surrogate Foley in a way which seems to apply to all cases of this kind: 'We see these claimants come in hopeful, some of them deluded in the belief they are related to the decedent, some of them distantly related, and yet barred under our statute of inheritance and distribution from participating in the estate because there are others nearer of kin. We see another type, where the evidence is fabricated.' The estate was divided among ten of the claimants, only one of whom knew of her existence. None had ever met her.

In 1904 an Irish gentleman farmer left an estate in England to his housekeeper, but the income from it was to go to his illegitimate son. The latter died ten years ago and the estate was sold for a very considerable sum, but the search for the heirs of the housekeeper continues here and in Ireland. The most careful checking of hundreds of entries at the appropriate

General Register Offices coupled with on-the-spot inquiries is often the only way in which these problems can be solved.

Clauses like that in the Will of the Revd Timothy Hargrove of Edmonton, Middlesex, bequeathing all his East India Annuities 'unto my second cousins on my father's side in Lancashire and elsewhere' (1793) are calculated to cause difficulties, and it was one in the will of William Jermy of Bayfield in Norfolk, made in 1751, which bequeathed his estates to two of his wife's nephews and, failing their male heirs, 'to such male person of the name of Jermy as shall be the nearest related to me in blood' which caused the Lord Chief Justice to say in 1878, 'There probably never was a property in the country the title of which has given rise to such obstinate disputes, or has been the source of so much litigation and crime.' The relations of the nephews, who died without issue, retained the estate contrary to the terms of the Will and bought off the Jermy claimants for £20 each, but the descendants of the latter continued to bring claims against the occupiers who successfully pleaded that they were covered by the Statute of Limitations. In 1922 the *Evening News* reported that one of the Jermy descendants believed that he should have inherited about three million pounds. In 1924 the *Daily Herald* published a similar story and the amount had increased to seven millions. In 1955 the *Eastern Daily Press* published an account under the heading 'The Jermy Millions', but followed it later with 'The Jermy Pence' after receiving information from a descendant of the occupiers.

The way in which the value of this estate was magnified is typical of many stories of the same kind. In a pamphlet put out by the Supreme Court Pay Office about 'Dormant Funds in Court' there is the following warning:

> The public are cautioned against relying upon the statements of persons styling themselves 'unclaimed money agents', at home or abroad, and professing to be able to recover money in Chancery on payment of fees or percentage, or to act on behalf of the 'Court of Chancery'. The Supreme Court of

Judicature has no such agents. The public are also cautioned against subscribing to syndicates formed, usually overseas, to exploit claims to estates in this country. Frequently and especially from the United States of America and Commonwealth countries a number of fruitless enquiries, stimulated by 'enquiry bureaux' or 'unclaimed money agents', arise regarding some estate which either does not exist, or, if it exists, is known to be in the possession of its lawful owners. Such cases have been, for instance, the Hedges, Jennens, Page, Hyde, Sir Francis Drake, Edwardes (of New York) and Mrs Mullins (of Bath) estates. More recent cases are the Everingham, Hobbs, Pascoe, D'Aquilar and Jaques estates and the Bailey Millions. It is recommended that independent advice should be obtained before making a payment to any agency for information, searches, copies of advertisements, etc., in respect of money alleged to be in Court. Experience has shown that the information so supplied is often valueless.

When a person dies without making a will and there are no ascertainable next-of-kin, or leaves a will but those entitled to the legacies cannot be traced, administration of the funds may be granted to the Treasury Solicitor. Under the Trustee Act of 1925 the persons in charge of trust funds may when there is real doubt as to their ownership or there are conflicting claims, place them in the custody of the Supreme Court. Claims may be made against the Treasury Solicitor subject, in general, to the rules of limitation under the Limitation Act of 1939, i.e. providing they are brought within twelve years. That rule may only be broken if there has been fraud or the property is held in trust. Provision may be made in these cases for the dependants of the deceased, whether they are related to him or not, but generally if a person dies without leaving a will and no spouse, issue, adopted children, parents, grandparents, or descendants of parents or grandparents on either side survive the deceased, then the property goes to the Crown. The funds held by the Supreme Court are not subject to the Limitation Act and they are the ones generally called 'Dormant Funds'. The great majority of them are of small amount. In respect of funds of £50 or more, the majority do not exceed £150 and if the aggregate amount of these funds is divided by the number of accounts involved, an average of approximately £400 per account is produced. Lists of the accounts have been published from time to time and they may be inspected without charge in the Royal Courts of Justice in the Strand, London, WC2.

There are several firms which make it a practice to go through the lists of Dormant Funds and those being administered by the Treasury Solicitor and to search out the heirs. In a way they provide a form of public service by bringing possible claims to the attention of persons who would not otherwise know about them, but they normally ask for a third of the amount involved and are subject to much criticism as a result. Their speculative searches may be quite expensive, however, and for every case in which they succeed there must be many in which they fail.

The genealogist may often be asked to turn private detective in this way and to trace the living rather than the dead. Reginald Hine said, 'It is indeed a small world. It is getting smaller every day. Yet, if you want to find anybody in this absurdly small world it can cause you a deal of trouble.' Very often the finding of Aunt Ethel, who walked out of the house forty years ago and has not been seen since, is a relatively simple matter of searching the death indexes at the General Register Office armed with her date of birth, or if she is alive her marriage can be searched for and then the births of her children, and then their marriages, and so on. Success will depend on how common the surname is. If she is alive and you have the exact date and place of her birth so that she can be identified in their records, the Department of Health and Social Security, through its Liaison Officer at Newcastle upon Tyne, will forward a letter to her. The Missing Persons Bureau of the Salvation Army will take up such a problem if the disappearance has caused hardship in the family. The Women's

Section there, which deals with deserted wives and unmarried mothers, has dealt with about twenty-five thousand such cases in the last fifteen years.

Similar in a way to intestacy cases are those in which a title is involved. All sorts of extraordinary things are believed about the way in which titles in this country descend, not least that they can be sold or given away or left unclaimed for a younger brother to take at mere caprice. The succession to the great majority of peerages, however, is determined by the wording of the original grant of the title, of the Letters Patent as it is called, and ordinarily the title can only pass in the male line to some direct descendant of the first grantee. However, a 'special remainder' in the Patent may open the succession to any relative who may be named, and sometimes the succession is to the 'heirs general' which means the nearest relative whatever, whether male or female, unless the term is 'heirs male general'. In most cases the succession is limited to heirs male, but in the older Baronies which were conferred by writ of summons instead of by patent, and in Scotland in the cases of some higher peerages, it is open also to females. Baronets can never be females, though under a few patents the male issue of females can succeed. Where a female succession prevails in peerage cases it has the peculiar feature, except in Scotland, of avoiding primogeniture, and regarding all the daughters as coheirs when there is no male issue. In such cases the title is said to fall into abeyance between the daughters and their descendants, unless one dies without any or the Sovereign selects one as the recipient. Such cases are not covered by the Sex Discrimination Act, as the daughters of the late Lord Quibell of Scunthorpe and the 13th Baronet Dixie discovered in their appeals in 1976.

The situation is extremely complex, and when one peer dies his eldest son will succeed and receive a writ of summons to the House of Lords as a matter of course, but a more remote relative will be required to prove his claim, and this may involve considerable difficulty, for it is one thing to prove that you are the son of somebody, but quite another thing to prove that your father's elder brother, or some more remote relative, died without issue.

When the late Earl of Buckinghamshire died it was well known that his successor in the title would be a second cousin, a gentleman who received much publicity at the time because he was a corporation gardener at Southend. It was no easy matter for him to prove his claim and to show that an uncle of his, Augustus Charles Hobart-Hampden, known as 'Hobart Pasha', who married firstly in Malta a lady who died in Constantinople and then secondly in Vienna another who survived him, and who himself died intestate in Milan, an incurable romancer as his memoirs reveal, had no issue by either wife. However, he did so in the end with the aid of the Society of Genealogists.

Much more remote cousinships may cause insuperable problems although there may be little doubt who the ultimate heir is. One well-known case is that of the Barons Gardner, descendants of the first Baron, Admiral Sir Alan Gardner, who commanded under Howe and was M.P. for Westminster, being created a Baron in 1806. His grandson, the third Baron, died without male issue in 1883 and the title has been dormant since then. The son of his first cousin, who was probably the heir, assumed the title but took no steps to establish his right thereto (although the *St James's Gazette* for 13 November 1901 asserts that he actually took his seat in the House of Lords, introduced by Lord Wemyss!) before he died in 1889. His son, Alan Legge Gardner, lived latterly in poverty growing guava pears in the Uttar Pradesh State of India and had many descendants.

Alan Legge Gardner's claim was rivalled by that of a second cousin whose father was an artist at Ipswich, where he too had assumed the title and died in 1901. He based his claim upon an alleged irregularity in the marriage of his rival's grandfather with an Indian Begum. The claims have never been officially tested and the rivalry between the two branches continues. There have been several Indian marriages in the family and in 1956 the Indian district where Alan Legge Gardner lived was said to have sixty other Gardners living in it. The production and hearing of evidence in cases of this kind is an extremely expensive matter.

The tracing of the history or provenance of some completely inanimate object can call for as much genealogical technique and expertise as the tracing of a person. It was Hine again who 'had a client, for example, John Beagarie by name, who made two outstanding Bunyan finds. The first was the anvil which Bunyan acquired, on being disbanded from the army, in order to take up his trade as a tinker; it bore his name, the date 1647, and the name of his village, "Helstow". The second was an iron fiddle which also bore his name and place of origin in the same rare, aspirated form. It was my difficult but fascinating task to trace these discoveries back, decade by decade, and generation by generation; to establish their pedigree by affidavits and declarations of marine-store dealers, cottagers and farmers, so that Sir Leicester Harmsworth, in buying them for presentation to the Bunyan Museum at Bedford, might rest assured that they were genuine relics of the immortal dreamer.'

When someone wrote to me about an old silver spoon with the initials B. L. and the date 1693 on the handle and the tradition of a descent from John Ridd of *Lorna Doone* fame, I little thought that it would be found to be the baptismal spoon of an ancestor born that year whose mother was a Rudd or Ridd from that same area of Devon about which Blackmore wrote.

In 1954 the Birmingham Corporation Art Gallery acquired, with the aid of the National Art-Collections Fund, a fine portrait group by Sir Joshua Reynolds, entitled 'The Roffey Family'. All that Tom Taylor, in his *Life of Sir Joshua Reynolds*, knew about the sitters was: 'At seven he goes out to tea and cards at Mr Roffey's, of whom I know nothing but that Sir Joshua seems to have visited him a good deal.' The lack of information was a challenge to the late Russell Muirhead who, by a process of elimination, well known to genealogists, identified the sitter and his family, and showed from the family's wills their interest in paintings generally. This expertise was put to considerable use by the late Director of the National Portrait Gallery, Kingsley Adams, and is amply illustrated in his article 'Portraiture Problems and Genealogy' in *The Genealogist's Magazine* (1964).

In a much longer exercise, done on behalf of a prominent antique dealer, an attempt was made to identify all the subscribers to Thomas Chippendale's book on furniture design, *The Director* (1752), and to come to some conclusions about which other cabinet makers were directly influenced by his work and were copying his designs, and which gentlemen subscribers might also have purchased his products. The value of the furniture in the possession of the descendants of the latter might thus be considerably increased. Prior to this antique dealer's death some years ago we dated from arms and inscriptions all manner of beautiful things, from snuff boxes to Victorian paper sculpture, which he brought to my office in South Kensington.

Of course one cannot always believe what is inscribed on a portrait, as Kingsley Adams points out, or on a medal for that matter, for many are falsely engraved, as any collector will know, with spurious details. Again, a careful inspection of army records and the medal rolls by an experienced genealogist will often sort out the truth from the fiction. For a gentleman who collected corkscrews I have inspected the patents taken out by Samuel Henshall who took to inventing them in the eighteenth century, and for a group of young men in Florida who were rebuilding an ancient Rolls Royce car I have traced details of its owners and its original colour!

The dating of objects from the quartered coats of arms they bear may greatly increase the value of a piece of furniture or china, or add much to the knowledge of the history of a house. From its heraldry the Christchurch Gate at Canterbury, the main entrance to the Cathedral, has recently been shown to commemorate Arthur, Prince of Wales, the son of Henry VII, and again from its magnificent display of heraldry the recently restored Hylton Castle near Sunderland can be dated to the last few years of the fourteenth century.

There is one other use to which genealogy is now often put, and that is in connection with religion. That it can be used to show 'the incompatibility of social and ethnic groups', as some claim, I will not accept for one moment, although there are a number who would seek to use it in that way.

The words of the Saviour to Nicodemus are accepted in their literal sense by the Church of Jesus Christ of Latter-day Saints, generally known as the Mormons: 'Except a man be born of water and of the Spirit, he cannot enter into the kingdom of God.' They claim that the scriptures make no distinction between the living and the dead, and that the law is of universal application, exemption being granted only to children who die in infancy, having no sin to expiate. To provide a means of salvation to everyone, facilities are made available in their temples for the baptism of the deceased through living proxies. They claim that evidence that such work was performed in the early Christian church is found in the words of St Paul to the Corinthians: 'Else what shall they do which are baptised for the dead, if the dead arise not at all? why are they then baptised for the dead?' Moreover, the Mormon Church accepts as true testimony the claim of Joseph Smith that shortly after the dedication of the Kirtland Temple in Ohio in 1836 the resurrected prophet Elijah bestowed upon him and his co-worker the authority to institute this work for the dead on his behalf. Since the institution of this practice the Latter-day Saints have zealously searched the records of the world for the history of their ancestors, that their forefathers may receive through them the new gospel of Christ. When marriages are performed in a Mormon temple the ordinance is 'sealed' under the authority of the priesthood and the parties believe that they are being joined not for life only but for eternity. In the same way the entire family relationship may be held intact when sealed and children born of parents married in the temple retain their relationship to father and mother after death. Those born of parents not originally married in the temple but later so joined may be sealed to the parents either while living or when dead. Thus through living proxies the Mormons claim that whole families are bound in eternal relationships, and the gospel 'is preached in the spirit world to those who have died without a knowledge of it.'

In connection with this work the Mormon Church maintains in Salt Lake City an extensive genealogical organisation, and its world-wide microfilming programme which has done so much to preserve for posterity an incredible multitude of records is justly famous. All the members of the Church contribute to this work either financially or by the searches they themselves carry out. A Genealogical Society was founded in 1894 and its library and collections are open freely to the public, duplicates of the films being held in controlled conditions in a vault in the Rocky Mountains. In 1964 it was said that forty million pages of records had been filmed in the British Isles. The great computer-produced index of baptismal entries taken from these records, and containing about twenty-five million names, I have mentioned earlier. The growth of branch libraries in the States and throughout the world, with their inter-loan system, is slowly making this material much more easily accessible to those who cannot get to Salt Lake City.

Also tracing their ancestries for religious purposes are those who wish to marry into Jewish families but possess no known Jewish blood, believing that their acceptance into the family will be that much easier or, in extreme cases, only made possible if they find Jewish ancestry. I fear that such speculative searches are generally doomed to failure, as are those by the gentile widows of Jews who have been buried alongside their orthodox fathers and wish to join their husbands in due course.

Also in this unfortunate class of genealogical inquirer comes the despairing mother who wants her son in some school or college which gives better entrance terms to the kin of the founder, and so attempts to find some such relationship. Prior to the abolition in the last century of most of the benefits deriving from the bequests of such founders, like those of

Archbishop Chichele to All Souls College, Oxford, and William of Wykeham to Winchester College, there was considerable interest in 'founders' kin' and an incentive to falsify descents, but the chance now of finding such a descent and of deriving benefit from it by speculative searches seems particularly remote.

In a similar way the American lady who has her husband in cold storage because he expressed a wish to be buried in the place in England from which his ancestors came, although the name of the emigrant ancestor and his place of origin here is as yet unknown, may wait a very long time before he can finally be laid to rest!

Chapter 10

Genealogy as Pastime and Profession

It may be that I have given the impression throughout this book that anyone can go out and trace his pedigree and that although he may meet some difficulties along the way, perseverance will overcome them. I hope that I may have encouraged some to read a handbook on the subject and to go and try their hand at searches themselves, as I have no doubt that that is how the greatest satisfaction is derived from the subject. However, it cannot be stressed sufficiently that no one can sit down and read a book and thereby become an accomplished genealogist, or that by working solely on one's own family or dabbling a little in local history no one can obtain sufficient experience to undertake professional work. Donald Lines Jacobus, the able and forthright American genealogist, has said, 'It is sometimes said of a man who insists on acting as his own lawyer that he has a fool for a client, and too often the same observation is appropriate for a man who insists on being his own genealogist.' He adds, 'Many family histories have been produced by enthusiastic novices, whose enthusiasm is too often the only qualification they bring to the task. The man who would seek the advice or services of a trained expert in any other field of human activity, considers himself quite competent to compile a history of his family. Without previous experience, without knowledge of record sources of information, and often without the kind of mentality capable of handling and arranging the infinite detail of facts, names and dates, it is small wonder that his book, more often than not, is a hodgepodge of traditional statements, guesses, and misinterpreted and misplaced records, interspersed with actual proved facts. Occasionally, results are not much better when an incompetent professional is employed.'

Those who have been involved in the subject professionally for a little time realise again and again their frustrating limitations of knowledge and tend to specialise in particular periods, areas or subjects of research, calling on each other to a large extent during the course of a search. The amateur cannot do this and must attempt to develop each field of expertise as he goes along. However, he has some advantage over a professional in that he is dealing with perhaps only one or two families and can keep all the details of the problem fresh in his mind over a long period, whereas a professional may be dealing with several hundred families at the same time.

It is sometimes said of the amateur that he will always have the defects of a self-taught man; he does not pay much attention to what has been done or what is being done by others. The genealogist, in particular, has tended to work alone, to be possessive about the information he has found, and, if he is a professional, to be very jealous of the special expertise he possesses which may give him an advantage over his rivals. It may have something to do with this that the Society of Genealogists was not founded until 1911 and that local family history societies have not developed until the last few years.

When, in 1685, Henry Mordaunt, Earl of Peterborough, using the pseudonym Robert Halstead, published the first family history to be printed in England, *Succinct Genealogies of the Noble and Ancient Houses of Alno, Broc and Mordaunt*, Sir Henry Chauncy had already spent five years collecting material for his great *Historical Antiquities of Hertfordshire* which he was to publish in 1700. Sir Henry, busy in his practice as a lawyer, and living in the relatively remote Ardeley Castle in Hertfordshire, had many of the problems of the modern genealogist. He complains in the Preface to his History of his family problems, well known to the local gentry, which 'made my Soule restlesse; and me unfit for a Work that requir'd the most calme, quiet, and serene thoughts, free from all interruptions and disturbances; and also my whole time and study, to search old legier Books; ransack mouldy Parchments; and examine overworne and blind Records'. Not only that, but they cost money, and again he complains of 'the great Charge and Paines of searching offices, and transcribing the Charters and Grants'.

In 1907 William Blyth Gerish, a noted local historian in Hertfordshire, wrote a life of Sir Henry and commenting on these passages took the opportunity to make reference to 'the excessively high charges of archivists for record searching at this period, when all the national archives are practically in order and may be examined freely'. Three years later, prompted no doubt by such thoughts, Gerish wrote to *Notes and Queries* suggesting the formation of a Society of Genealogists. He was joined by Charles A. Bernau (who was already running a profitable research agency and was well known as the author of *The Genealogy of the Submerged*, one of the first books to be devoted entirely to the tracing of the ancestry of the common man), by Richard Holworthy and by George Sherwood, both professional genealogists, and a Society was founded in the office of the latter in the Strand in 1911, it being an 'Association not for profit'.

Their feelings and objects were expressed in a leaflet put out at the time. They believed:

> That societies established for the purpose of printing and distributing record material fail to a large extent in their object, if that be taken to include the ready discovery and verification of facts. A large sum of money is expended, and the result, in printed books of collections and transactions, lies stowed away on dusty shelves to which few possess the key or the knowledge requisite to ready access; the great majority has neither the leisure nor the opportunity to reach the vast stores of available material. The function of the Society of Genealogists is to collect, index, and arrange historical, genealogical, and heraldic evidence, for the use of its members. The Society has secured in London, in a

central and easily accessible position, offices to house a Reference Library, and from which the labours of genealogists, local historians, students of heraldry, etc., in all parts of the country, and indeed in all parts of the world, are being consolidated and directed. The intention is to avoid that over-lapping which is inevitable to isolated effort, as well as that somewhat unsatisfactory cultivation of detached fields of research so often pursued without any knowledge of what is being done and of what has been done by others to the same end. By the aid of Committees to effect desired objects, and by keeping Members informed of what those Committees are doing, much unnecessary labour must be saved.

The enthusiasm of the founder members was enormous, and a valuable library with vast document collections and card indexes was built up. When *The Genealogist* ceased publication the Society started its own periodical publication, *The Genealogists Magazine*, and this has been issued quarterly since 1925. It has never concerned itself with publishing family histories and pedigrees as such unless they were of wide interest or demonstrated some particular type of research or source. The June 1961 edition contains a detailed account of the special collections then in the Library, and an abbreviated account appears in *The Genealogists' Handbook*, a highly condensed guide to sources in the British Isles, five editions of which have been published by the Society. The Society is justly proud of its other publications, those listing its parish register copies, directories and poll books, and the parishes covered by the Marriage Index, forming a partial catalogue of the Library, for which there is also an outline Guide.

The membership of the Society was 419 in 1921, and was still less than a thousand in 1946. It had grown to 1,600 in 1960 and then mushroomed to the present figure of about five thousand. These members pay an annual subscription, but the library is also open to the public on payment of daily and half-daily fees. For many years there was a particular policy to keep the membership down, but the growing need for money to house the collections, particularly after the move to the present headquarters at 37 Harrington Gardens, London SW7, in 1954, altered all that, membership was encouraged, and the club atmosphere which existed in the first few years after the move has now, perhaps unfortunately, almost gone. However, through lectures and courses, meetings and the Magazine, there is plenty of opportunity to meet others interested in the same fields and to exchange information, and all are welcomed, from the complete beginner to the professional.

There is always a certain amount of rivalry between the amateur and the professional but it has been the Society's strength that what has been done has been done for the benefit of all without distinction. There is a very small research department which undertakes a very limited amount of work for members who cannot come to the rooms and for non-members, but the correspondence received by the Society is vast and with a very limited staff it is unfortunately not possible to answer every letter individually. Those enclosing a stamped and addressed envelope, however, do receive better attention! For those who cannot carry out their own searches the Society can provide a list of professionals in various parts of the country who have been recommended to it by its members for work of this kind.

The last few years has seen a quite new development in English genealogy with the foundation of many county family history societies, some of which are extremely active in the transcription and indexing of local material. Their journals reveal a great enthusiasm and their local functions clearly provide a meeting place for all interested in the subject whether they live in that area or have ancestors from it. These societies are all members of the Federation of Family History Societies which was formed in 1974 and which, through its Secretary, Mrs Elizabeth Simpson, has since that date done an enormous amount to encourage amateur genealogists in this country, to put them on the right lines in their studies, and to co-ordinate their work. More will be achieved through their valuable *Family History News and Digest*, which commenced publication in 1977. The Secretary will provide a list of all the local societies in the British Isles on receipt of a stamped and addressed envelope (or of course International Reply Coupons from those living abroad) at 2 Stella Grove, Tollerton, Nottinghamshire.

Because there is a widespread interest in genealogy there is a common belief that professional genealogists must be making a great deal out of it, but that I have always greatly doubted. Certainly where publication is concerned he will not make money. In the view of Donald Lines Jacobus, 'No genealogy published today, if the work has been properly and thoroughly done, can produce a monetary profit.' It is eighty years since Sir William Fraser – 'not a very able man' in the view of his fellow Scottish genealogist, Sir James Balfour Paul – left over £100,000 mainly made out of genealogy, having been paid about £2000 each for the many family histories he wrote, but I know of no twentieth-century equivalent. It is not the amount which one charges for an hour's work which is the sole consideration in these matters, and one's income is conditioned by the number of free hours that are available for paying work after dealing with the correspondence, much of it quite unproductive, which any successful practice in genealogy generates. Practically all the professionals I know are supplementing an income from some other source, and there is certainly no 'career' in it. The number of professionals employing others, and consequently the number of openings, is extremely small.

We all know that it is quite impossible to estimate the length of time likely to be taken in tracing a pedigree, or to say if it is possible to trace a pedigree at all. For this reason most professional genealogists now ask for sufficient money to cover about one or two days' work in advance, or authority to proceed for a longer time, and then give a report of all their findings. This report may quite likely not contain anything in actual tabular pedigree form, but it will, I hope, contain an exact account of all the research procedures which have been gone through, together with the appropriate references and places of deposit of the records consulted. Certified copies of parish register entries and of other documents, such as wills, will not normally be provided unless specifically asked for by the client. The charge for a day's work will normally include small out-of-pocket expenses and the client is generally asked to pay for only a proportion of the travelling time and expenses when routine journeys are made, say in the case of a London searcher to and from the General Register Office and the Public Record Office, where it should be possible to spread the charge over several clients.

Now that there is a fairly good network of genealogists and record agents covering most of the country there is little excuse for the genealogist to travel extensively, and few now do. You may thus depend that a genealogist who advertises his services in any part of the kingdom is either travelling at your expense or sub-contracting the work to another genealogist with a special knowledge of the area required. This is not to say that there are not times when it is preferable to have the same person conducting the whole research from beginning to end, but this may now be a luxury and it is certainly here that the amateur conducting all his own searches has the advantage. The private genealogist working for a small number of clients may be the answer, and he will certainly have a greater pride in his work, give more individual attention and establish a personal relationship with his client, in a way which the larger firm of professionals may have difficulty in equalling. However, the man who has specialised in Norfolk sources all his life will be all at sea at the General Register Office and the Public Record Office, and a large professional organisation, like the College of Arms, may well be able to draw on specialists in all areas, periods and subjects, in a way quite unknown to the local man.

How then does the client choose his genealogist? I have mentioned the list maintained by the Society of Genealogists, but in 1968 was formed the Association of Genealogists and Record Agents. This Association (address: 123 West End Road, Ruislip, Middlesex) is open only to well qualified persons of considerable practical experience, and the members have for the most part been actively engaged as genealogists or record agents for a number of years. It has published several lists of its members with notes as to the regions they serve ranging from central London to the Isle of Man, and of their specialised knowledge and interests, which range from medieval Latin to East Prussian families. The Association has a machinery for investigating the complaints of any client and I cannot stress sufficiently that anyone wishing to employ a professional should use a member of that organisation. In North America the same would apply to the Board for the Certification of Genealogists which was established in Washington in 1964. Of course there are able genealogists of long standing and high repute in both countries who would not dream of applying for membership of either organisation, and as genealogists tend to be individualists there is little one can do about it. The client of such a one, however, should realise that he will have practically no redress should anything go wrong or the finished work be unsatisfactory. I should perhaps mention here that any genealogist who is a member of the Society can advertise in *The Genealogists' Magazine* but the Society may have no knowledge of his work and takes no responsibility for it.

I have myself summarised the aims of the Association of Genealogists and Record Agents when it was founded as to establish standards of competence in the various skills and techniques of professional genealogists and record agents, and to maintain a public register arranged by subject, period and locality of those considered to have attained those standards. Also to establish a standard of ethics for their conduct in relation to their clients, towards each other, and to the record repositories which they use. Also to encourge improved methods in the presentation of the results of their research, and to establish minimum scales of charges for work in their various fields. And finally to represent the profession in matters relating to the conditions of their work and the records they use, and to serve as a link between them for the general interchange and expression of their views. The Association has already achieved a great deal with very limited resources and owes much to its Secretary, Miss Isobel Mordy. Copies of the code of ethics to which members subscribe can be obtained, and its other activities are chronicled in the *Newsletter*.

The ultimate in genealogical studies in recent years has been the development of a group of persons who are interested in all the references to one specific surname and its variants. They attempt to build up pedigrees of all the families of this name and to collect all the available material about them. A register of these 'One-Name Studies' is maintained by the Federation of Family History Societies.

Where several persons have been interested in the one name they have often joined together and founded family associations with newsletters and annual reunions. Such societies have been frequent in the United States of America but have not had a very long history in England. At least that was what I believed until I found the following invitation card in the Document Collection at the Society of Genealogists, 'A General Meeting of the Surname of KING, being Appointed to be Held at Mr. John King's at the Rummer Tavern in White-Chappel, London, on Saturday the 29th of this Instant May, 1703, being the Anniversary in Memory of the happy Restoration of KING CHARLES the 2d. and the ROYAL Family. You are ernestly desired to be there by Twelve of the Clock precisely, by your most humble Servants, Robert King, Gent., James King, Herald Painter, John King, Vintner, Stewards. Pay for the Ticket 2s. 6d. and bring it for your Admittance'.

As I have said, the amateur has many advantages over the professional. The latter is all the while restricted in his activities by the funds available and thus has always to limit the time he takes in any search. He cannot afford to browse or let his eye stray from the work in hand. The amateur, however, can develop whatever line of enquiry takes his fancy, he can let his imagination run riot, and he can begin to explore some of the myriad highways and byways of history.

He will find that a day reading old newspapers goes like

a flash if he once lets himself look at the advertisements, that revealing court records once picked up cannot be put down, that the census returns take him into a different world, and, if he is lucky, that wills and other records will sketch in the characters and private lives of his ancestors until he feels that he is almost trespassing on their privacy.

Where facts and records fail, a reasonable amount of surmise, probability and imagination will help to fill the gaps. There are, after all, as we have seen, plenty of good precedents for the use of imagination! Uther Pendragon, the father of King Arthur, may not have existed. Heraldry in his day was quite unknown. But so what? Robert Glover, Somerset Herald in the sixteenth century, who evidently had a rich fancy, ascribed to him arms of which he would undoubtedly have been proud: 'On a gold shield two green wiverns with red crowns but without legs respecting each other'.

Bibliographical Notes

There is a good general bibliography in G. K. Hamilton-Edwards, *In search of Ancestry*, Chichester, 1974, and this may be supplemented by H. G. Harrison, *A Select Bibliography of English Genealogy*, London, 1937, the county sections of which have been brought up to date in C. R. Humphery-Smith, *A Genealogist's Bibliography*, Chichester, 1976. See also P. W. Filby, *American & British Genealogy & Heraldry: a selected list of books*, American Library Association, Chicago, 1975.

Examples used in this book which are not mentioned in the following notes are generally from unpublished sources.

Foreword and Chapter 1

Lord Mountbatten's remarks appear in *Genealogist's Magazine*, xii (1957), 367. For comments on President Grant's false ancestry see *National Genealogical Society Quarterly*, lxiv (1976), 72. The impact of *Roots* in the United States is described by Mark Ottaway in 'Tangled Roots', in *Sunday Times*, 10 April 1977.

The comments by Goethe appear in Romain Rolland, *Goethe and Beethoven*, New York, 1931, and those on the search for Jewish ancestry for the Aryans in a letter from Col. J. C. Wedgwood in *Genealogists' Magazine*, vii (1935), 121.

Chapter 2

For general guides to the available sources see P. Spufford and A. J. Camp, *The Genealogists' Handbook*, London, 1969; A. J. Camp, *Tracing Your Ancestors*, London, 1972; A. J. Willis, *Genealogy for Beginners*, Chichester, 1976; and G. K. Hamilton-Edwards, *In Search of Ancestry*, Chichester, 1974. See also the Society of Genealogists' leaflets, *Family Records & Their Layout* (No. 3, 1977) and *Note Taking and Keeping for Genealogists* (No. 4, 1977).

For the National Pedigree Index see *Genealogists' Magazine*, xviii (1976), 327.

For recent memory and family papers see D. J. Steel and L. Taylor, *Family History in Schools*, London, 1973.

For the Registrar General's records see D. E. Gardner and F. Smith, *Genealogical Research in England and Wales*, i (1956), 46–83, and *The Story of the General Register Office and its Origins from 1538 to 1937*, H.M.S.O., 1937. For the Census Returns see Gardner and Smith, *op. cit.*, i, 84–117. For Directories see J. E. Norton, *Guide to Directories*, Royal Historical Society, 1950, and L. W. L. Edwards, *A New and Revised Catalogue of Directories and Poll Books in the Possession of the Society of Genealogists*, London, 1973.

For Parish Registers see D. J. Steel, *National Index of Parish Registers*, i, (1976), 'Sources for Births, Marriages & Deaths before 1837'. For the whereabouts of original registers see Local Population Studies, *Original Parish Registers in Record Offices and Libraries*, Matlock, 1974, and its *First Supplement*, Matlock, 1976. For the whereabouts of copies see Society of Genealogists, *Parish Register Copies: Part 1, The Society of Genealogists' Collection*, London, 1975, and *Part 2, Other Collections*, London, 1974. For the consolidated indexes see R. W. Massey, *A List of Parishes in Boyd's Marriage Index*, London, 1974; Genealogical Society of Utah, *Parish and Vital Records Listings*, Salt Lake City, 1976; and *Pallot's Marriage and Birth Indexes – Guide to Parishes*,

Institute of Heraldic and Genealogical Studies, Canterbury, n. d.

For churchyard inscriptions see H. L. White, *Monuments and their Inscriptions*, London, 1977, and for parish records see W. E. Tate, *The Parish Chest*, Cambridge, 1967, and John West, *Village Records*, London 1962. The Cowden examples come from R. Hine, *Relics of an Un-common Attorney*, London, 1951, 97–101.

For the nonconformists see D. J. Steel, *National Index of Parish Registers*, ii (1973), 'Sources for Nonconformist Genealogy & Family History', and iii (1974), 'Sources for Roman Catholic & Jewish Genealogy & Family History', and for the list of their records now at the Public Record Office, *Lists of Non-parochial Registers and Records in the custody of the Registrar General*, H.M.S.O., 1859.

For probate records generally see the introduction to A. J. Camp, *Wills and Their Whereabouts*, London, 1974. For the Principal and District Probate Registries, pp. 187–19, for the Estate Duty Office, pp. 80–81, for the Prerogative Court of Canterbury, pp. 72–79, and for Inventories, pp. xviii–xix, of that work.

For a bibliography of apprentices see *Genealogists' Magazine*, vii (1935), 18 and 74. For those in London see three articles in that *Magazine*, 'Genealogical Material in the Guildhall Records' by A. H. Thomas, ii (1926), 45–48, 'The Guildhall Library in War and Peace' by R. Smith, x (1948), 175–9, and 'Genealogy and the City of London Records' by P. E. Jones, xi (1951–2), 133–6 and 167–73, and for the Index maintained by the City Chamberlain, M. T. Medlycott, 'The City of London Freedom Registers', xix (1977), 45–7 and 141–2.

For printed school registers see P. M. Jacobs, *Registers of the Universities, Colleges and Schools of Great Britain and Ireland: a List*, London, 1964.

For army ancestors see the Public Record Office leaflet *British Military Records as sources for Biography and Genealogy*, and C. T. and M. J. Watts, 'In Search of a Soldier

Ancestor', in *Genealogists' Magazine*, xix (1977), 125–8. For those in the navy see the Public Record Office leaflet *Records of the Registrar General of Shipping and Seamen*, and R. D. Merriman, 'Naval Records', in *Genealogists' Magazine*, x (1947), 95–104. The 'Trinity House Petitions' are described by E. P. Stapleton in that *Magazine*, vi (1934), 490–2.

For the professions generally see Chapters 11–14, of G. K. S. Hamilton-Edwards, *In Search of Ancestry*, Chichester, 1974, and for the examples of successive generations see a series of articles in *Genealogists' Magazine*, vi (1933–4), 189, 402–5, 452–3 and 493, and ix (1942), 227.

For biographical dictionaries and official lists see P.M. Riches, *An Analytical Bibliography of Universal Collected Biography*, 1934; 'County Biographical Dictionaries, 1890–1937', in *Bulletin of Institute of Historical Research*, xxxiv (1961), 55; and 'Bibliographical Guide to the Lists of English Office-holders (to c. 1800)', in F. M. Powicke and E. B. Fryde, *Handbook of British Chronology*, Royal Historical Society, London, 1961.

For newspapers see D. J. Steel, *National Index of Parish Registers*, i (1976), 271–91, and C. D. P. Nicholson, 'The Genealogical Value of the Early English Newspapers', in *Genealogists' Magazine*, v (1929), 14–7, 48–51, 71–2 and 111–4.

County records generally are described in W. G. Hoskins, *Local History in England*, 1959, and F. G. Emmison, *Archives and Local History*, 1965.

For the Protestation and Association Oath Rolls see 'The Protestation Returns of 1641–2: a checklist of printed and other sources', by L. W. L. Edwards, in *Genealogists' Magazine*, xix (1977), 84–5, and Wallace Gandy, *The Association Oath Rolls of 1696*, London, 1921.

For Poll Books see the note on Directories above.

For manorial records see N. J. Hone, *The Manor and Manorial Records*, 1925, and for a general survey of the Public Records see V. H. Galbraith, *An Introduction to the Use of the Public Records*, London, 1952, the series of articles by R. E.

Latham, 'Hints on Interpreting the Public Records', in *Amateur Historian*, i, (1952–3), and *Short Guides to Records* published by the Historical Association. The Star Chamber computer-compiled index is T. G. Barnes, *List and Index to the Proceedings in Star Chamber for the Reign of James I*, 3 vols., American Bar Foundation, 1975.

For problems with handwriting see F. G. Emmison, *How to Read Local Archives 1550–1700*, 1968; L. C. Hector, *The Handwriting of English Documents*, 1966, and H. E. P. Grieve, *Examples of English Handwriting 1150–1750*, 1959. For abbreviated forms and Latin see C. T. Martin, *The Record Interpreter*, 1910, and E. A. Gooder, *Latin for Local History*, 1961. For the early period, John Unett, *Making a Pedigree*, Newton Abbot, 1971, has some good examples.

For Ireland see Rosemary ffolliott, *A Simple Guide to Irish Genealogy*, London, 1966, and Margaret Falley, *Irish and Scotch-Irish Ancestral Research*, 2 vols., Evanston, 1961.

For Scotland see G. K. Hamilton-Edwards, *In Search of Scottish Ancestry*, Chichester, 1972; D. Whyte, *Introducing Scottish Genealogical Research*, Kirkliston, 1977, and A. Sandison, *Tracing Ancestors in Shetland*, Lerwick, 1972.

For India see Sir William Foster, *Guide to the India Office Records, 1600–1858*, London, 1920. For civil registration in the Commonwealth see *Abstract of Arrangements respecting registration of births, marriages and deaths in the United Kingdom and the other countries of the British Commonwealth of Nations, and in the Irish Republic*, H.M.S.O., London, 1952, and for registers returned to England see *Parish Registers: a Handlist: Part III: Provisional Guide to . . . Registers . . . of Anglican Communities Abroad forming part of the archives of the Diocese of London*, The Guildhall Library, London, 1967.

For sources in America see G. H. Doane, *Searching for your Ancestors*, Minneapolis, 1973, and M. Rubincam and J. Stephenson, *Genealogical Research Methods and Sources*, American Society of Genealogists, Washington, 1960. For Canada see *Tracing Your Ancestors in Canada*, Public Archives of Canada, Toronto, Ottawa, 1972. For South Africa see R. T. J. Lombard, *Handbook for Genealogical Research in South Africa*, Human Sciences Research Council, Pretoria, 1977. For Australia and New Zealand see Nancy Gray, *Compiling Your Family History*, Society of Australian Genealogists, Sydney, 1965; A. G. Peake, *Sources for South Australian Family History*, South Australian Genealogy and Heraldry Society, Adelaide, 1977; and N. T. Hansen, *Guide to Genealogical Sources: Australia and New Zealand*, Melbourne, 1962.

Chapter 3

For Thomas Snell see A. J. Willis, *Winchester Consistory Court Depositions 1561–1602*, Folkestone, 1960, 31. For mobility see P. Spufford, *Four Centuries of population movement within Great Britain: the seventeenth century*, World Conference on Records and Genealogical Seminar, Salt Lake City, 1969. For settlement certificates see W. E. Tate, *The Parish Chest*, Cambridge, 1967, and James Burrow, *A series of the decisions of the Court of King's Bench upon Settlement-Cases, 1732–1776*, 2 vols., London, 1768–82.

For the growth of London see E. A. Wrigley, 'A simple model of London's importance in changing English society and economy 1650–1750' in *Past and Present*, xxvii (1967), 44, also N. G. Brett-James, *The Growth of Stuart London*, London and Middlesex Archaeological Society, 1935, 498, and S. Jenkins, *Landlords to London: the story of a capital and its growth*, London, 1975.

For the percentage of Will leavers see A. J. Camp, *Wills and their whereabouts*, London, 1974, xxxvi–xxxviii.

For mobility at Sheffield see E. J. Buckatzsch, 'Places of origin of a group of immigrants into Sheffield 1624–1799', in *Economic History Review*, 2nd Series, ii (1950), 303–6.

For land registration in Yorkshire see J. N. Thompson, 'The Yorkshire Deeds Registries', in *Association of Genealogists and Record Agents: Newsletter*, No. 15 (1977), 3–6.

For London apprentices see references quoted above, Chapter 2.

For surnames in Bow Creek see B. S. Bramwell, 'Frequency of Cousin Marriages', in *Genealogists' Magazine*, viii (1939), 305–16. For the Atherton family see R. S. Atherton, '*Beyond* the workhouse', in *Genealogists' Magazine*, xvii (1973), 261–5.

For adoption see Angela Hamblin and Alan Neale, *The Other Side of Adoption*, London, 1977, and Isobel Mordy, 'Adopted People', in *Association of Genealogists and Record Agents: Newsletter*, No. 15 (1977), 6-8, and for the Legitimacy Acts the same *Newsletter*, No. 16 (1977), 4-5. For Mrs Fitzherbert's adoptions see W. H. Wilkins, *Mrs Fitzherbert and George IV*, 2 vols., London, 1905, and for Frances Stevenson's daughter see A. J. P. Taylor, *My darling Pussy: the letters of Lloyd George and Frances Stevenson*, 1975.

Chapter 4

For the records of immigrants see R. F. Monger, 'Immigrants in the Public Records', in *Genealogists' Magazine*, xvi (1970), 197-201.

For the Jews see D. J. Steel and E. R. Samuel, *National Index of Parish Registers*, iii (1974), 957-976, and for the Isaac family of Patrixbourne, W. G. Davis, *The Ancestry of Mary Isaac*, Portland, Maine, 1955, 3-5.

For the Huguenots see S. Minet, 'Huguenot Records', in *Genealogists' Magazine*, xii (1956), 149-154, 185-188, and C. E. Lart, 'The Huguenot Society and its Work', in *Genealogists' Magazine*, iii (1927), 50-53.

For the problems of tracing emigrants back into England see 'Genealogical Research in England' in C. E. Banks, *Topographical Dictionary of 2886 English Emigrants to New England 1620-1650*, Baltimore, 1969, xiii-xxix, and 'Getting Ready to cross the Atlantic' in G. H. Doane, *Searching for your Ancestors,* Minneapolis, 1973, and J. L. Druse, *Through Parish and Probate to your English Ancestry,* Detroit Society for Genealogical Research, 1965. For other records of emigration see R. F. Monger, 'Emigrants in Public Records', in *Genealogists' Magazine,* xvi (1969), 135-143, and P. A. M. Taylor, 'Passenger Lists as an Historical Source', in *Genealogists' Magazine* xii (1956), 197-200, and M. J. Burchall, 'Parish-Organised Emigration to America: 19th Century Examples from East Sussex', in *Genealogists' Magazine,* xviii (1976), 336-42.

Chapter 5

For the ancestry of Lord Snowdon see A. R. Wagner, 'Ancestry of Mr Antony Armstrong-Jones', in *Genealogists' Magazine,* xiii (1959-61), 97-103, 129-133, 280-1; for that of President Kennedy see *Burke's Presidential Families of the United States of America,* London, 1975, 544.

For the descendants of the Magna Carta barons see 'Representation of the "Magna Carta" Barons' in *Genealogists' Magazine,* viii (1938), 206-9. For the companions of William the Conqueror see Walter Rye, 'An Index to six various versions of the so-called Roll of Battle Abbey', in *Genealogists' Magazine,* i-v (1925-30), also 'Companions of the Conqueror', in *Genealogists' Magazine,* vi (1932), 50-57, and (by G. H. White) ix (1944), 417-24, also D. C. Douglas, 'Companions of the Conqueror', in *History,* xxviii (1944), 129-47, and C. Morton and H. Muntz, *The Carmen de Hastingae Proelio of Guy Bishop of Amiens,* Oxford, 1972.

For the Malet descent see G. E. G. Malet, 'The Origin of the Malets of Enmore', in *Genealogists' Magazine,* viii (1939), 316-24, and for other early descents see A. R. Wagner, *English Genealogy,* Oxford, 1972, 9-90.

For the descendants of Edward III see the Marquis of Ruvigny and Raineval, *The Blood Royal of Britain,* 1903, and

The Plantagenet Roll of the Blood Royal, 4 vols., 1905–8. For those of Mary Queen of Scots see A. C. Addington, *The Royal House of Stuart*, 3 vols., London, 1969-76. For those of Nell Gwyn see D. Adamson and P. B. Dewar, *The House of Nell Gwyn: the fortunes of the Beauclerk family 1670-1974*, London, 1974.

For the royal descent of Lord Snowdon see *Genealogists' Magazine*, xiii (1960), 132, of Mark Phillips see *Genealogists' Magazine*, xvii (1973), 418, of American Presidents see the Review in *National Genealogical Society Quarterly*, lxiv (1976), 71-2, by Milton Rubincam of *Burke's Presidential Families of the United States of America*, London, 1975, Appendix C, 'Presidents of Royal Descent', pp. 607-624.

For the quartiers of Edward VII see G. W. Watson, *The 4096 Quartiers of King Edward VII*, Exeter, 1904, reprinted from *The Genealogist*, New Series, xvi-xx (1899-1904); of the Prince of Wales see Gerald Paget, *The Lineage and ancestry of H. R. H. Prince Charles, Prince of Wales*, 2 vols., Edinburgh, 1977; of the Queen Consorts see *The Genealogist*, New Series, vi-xii (1890-1896); of the Queen Mother see *Genealogists' Magazine*, ix (1940), 7-13.

For the matrilineal descent of Queen Victoria see *Genealogists' Magazine*, iii (1927), 6-9, xiii (1960), 241-4, xiv (1964), 273-7. For Charlemagne and St Arnulf see *New England Historical Genealogical Register*, ci (1947), 109-12. For princess Zaida see *The American Genealogist*, xxxviii (1962), 245–8, xxxix (1963), 157–160, lii (1967), 32, and for the other Moorish ancestors of Isabel of Castile see W. H. Turton, *The Plantagenet Ancestry*, Baltimore, 1968, tables 44 and 45, and *The Augustan*, xii (1969), 217–23.

For the descents from the ancient world see A. R. Wagner, *Pedigree and Progress: Essays in the genealogical interpretation of history*, London, 1975, and for Pierre Dolgorouky's comment his *Notice sur les principales Familles de la Russie*, Brussels, 1843, 55.

Chapter 6

For the claims of Ruvigny see A. R. Wagner, *English Genealogy*, Oxford, 1972, 234, and C. E. Lart, *Huguenot Pedigrees*, London, 1924, vol. i, 76-83; of Brydges see A. R. Wagner, *op. cit.*, 359, quoting G. F. Beltz, *A Review of the Chandos Peerage Case*, 1834; and of Plantagenet Harrison see A. R. Wagner, *op. cit.*, 359.

For Swale and Lawson see *Complete Baronetage*, ed. G.E.C,. iii (1903), 46-7, and iv (1904), 19-21; and *Whitaker's Peerage*, 1913; and *Debrett's Peerage*, 1920; and G. S. H. L. Washington, *Prince Charlie and the Bonapartes*, Cambridge, 1960, 21 and 68.

For Paver see *Herald and Genealogist*, iii (1866), 266-73, 464–5; *Genealogists' Magazine*, viii (1939), 333–4, 398; *New England Historical and Genealogical Register*, xi (1857), 259–71; *Dictionary of National Biography*, xliv (1895), 101–2. For T. C. Banks and Frederic Boase, *Modern English Biography*, London, 1892, i, 152-3, and *Dictionary of National Biography*, iii (1885), 134–6. For Humphrys see *Complete Peerage*, xii, pt. i (1953), Appendix G, 14–17.

For Radclyffe see W. H. Godfrey, A. R. Wagner and H. S. London, *The College of Arms*, London Survey Committee, 1963, 217; *Gentleman's Magazine*, xc (1820), i, 268-9.

For Dethick see Godfrey, Wagner and London, *op. cit.*, 47-8; *Dictionary of National Biography*, xiv (1888), 419-20. For Dering see J. H. Round, *Peerage and Pedigree*, 1910, ii, 113-6.

For Harrison see J. P. Earwaker, *A Lancashire Pedigree Case: a History of the various trials for the recovery of the Harrison Estates from 1873 to 1886*, Warrington, 1887. For the Tracy peerage see *The Complete Peerage*, xii, pt. ii (1959), 5. For Herbert Davies see W. P. W. Phillimore, *The 'Principal Genealogical Specialist'; or Regina v. Davies and the Shipway Genealogy, being the story of a remarkable pedigree fraud*, London, 1899. For W. S. Spence see R. Stewart-Brown,

'The Cotgreave Pedigree Forgeries', in *Genealogist's Magazine*, vi (1933), 288–93, and the references to *Notes & Queries* there cited.

Chapter 7

For the sale of false arms see *The Heraldry Gazette*, ii, Nos. 47-8 (1968) and A. R. Wagner, 'Some Aspects of Heraldry' in *Genealogists' Magazine*, vii (1936), 217. For John Izzard Pryor see Gerald Curtis, *A chronicle of small beer*, Chichester, 1970, 182, and J. E. Cussans, *History of Hertfordshire; Hundred of Broadwater*, 1877, 40.

For Heraldry generally see A. R. Wagner, *Heraldry in England*, London, 1946; C. and A. Lynch-Robinson, *Intelligible Heraldry*, London, 1948; I. Moncreiffe and D. Pottinger, *Simple Heraldry*, London, 1953; A. C. Fox-Davies, *The Complete Guide to Heraldry*, London, 1949 (revised by J. P. Brooke-Little, 1969); *Boutell's Heraldry*, 3rd ed. 1864, or modern eds, by C. W. Scott-Giles and J. P. Brooke-Little, 1950 and later.

Examples of modern grants come from Lt. Col. Gayre of Gayre and Nigg, *The Armorial Who is Who 1961-62*, Edinburgh, 1962; of supporters and badges from Fox-Davies, *op. cit.*, 401-440, 453-470; of the Hay arms from Fox-Davies, *op. cit.*, 415, quoting J. Balfour-Paul, *Heraldry in relation to Scottish History and Art*, Edinburgh, 1899.

For the Heralds see A. R. Wagner, *Heralds and Heraldry in the Middle Ages*, Oxford, 1956 and his *Heralds of England*, H.M.S.O., 1967; and for their records, A. R. Wagner, *Records and Collections of the College of Arms*, London, 1952. For the 892 quarters of the Duke of Northumberland see *Herald and Genealogist*, iii (1886), 268.

For the Court of the Earl Marshal see G. D. Squibb, *The High Court of Chivalry*, London, 1959, and his *Report of Heraldic Cases in the Court of Chivalry 1623-1732*, London,

1956. For the deputy heralds see A. R. Wagner and G. Squibb, 'Deputy Heralds', in F. Emmison and R. Stephens, *Tribute to an Antiquary*, London, 1976, 229-264. For William Oldys see Godfrey, Wagner and London, *op. cit.*, 115-6, and *Dictionary of National Biography*, xlii (1895), 119-23. For the later heralds see A. R. Wagner, *English Genealogy*, Oxford, 1972, 400-403.

For the Corporation of Manchester's case see *The Full Report of the Case of the Mayor, Alderman and Citizens of the City of Manchester versus the Manchester Palace of Varieties Limited in the High Court of Chivalry on Tuesday, 21st December 1954*, The Heraldry Society, 1955, and *The Heraldry Gazette*, No. 61, March, 1975.

Chapter 8

For surnames generally see P. H. Reaney, *The Origin of English Surnames*, 1967, and *A Dictionary of British Surnames*, 1961. For names collected by Hine see R. L. Hine, *Confessions of an Un-common Attorney*, London, 1945, 76. For aliases see F. Leeson, 'Aliases', in *Genealogists' Magazine*, xv (1968), 594-9, and 'Alternative Surnames' in D. J. Steel, *National Index of Parish Registers*, London, 1976, i, 92-6.

For the Northern Ireland surname project see G. B. Adams and B. S. Turner, 'A family name survey of Northern Ireland', in H. Voitl, *The Study of the Personal Names of the British Isles*, Erlangen, 1976, 114–118. R. A. McKinley, 'The Survey of English Surnames', is also in Voitl, *op. cit.*, 119–25. For the law as to changes of name see introduction to W. P. W. Phillimore and E. A. Fry, *An Index of Changes of Name 1760-1901*, Baltimore, 1968.

For christian names generally see 'Christian Names' in D. J. Steel, *National Index of Parish Registers*, London, 1976, i, 101–28; the introduction to E. G. Withycombe, *Oxford*

Dictionary of English Christian Names, 1950, and D. J. Steel, 'The Descent of Christian Names', in *Genealogists' Magazine*, xiv (1962), 34-43. For Jewish customs see E. R. Samuel, 'Jewish Naming Customs', in *Genealogists' Magazine*, xiv (1962), 44-7.

Chapter 9

For the British Record Society see Peter Spufford, 'The British Record Society – Eighty Years of an Index', in *The Indexer*, Spring, 1968, and 'Marc Fitch and the British Record Society' in F. Emmison and R. Stephens, *Tribute to an Antiquary*, London, 1976, 9-19. For genealogy and history see P. Spufford, 'Genealogy and the Historian', in *The Genealogists' Magazine*, xv (1967), 431–47; and demography see D. J. Steel, 'Genealogy and Demography', in *Genealogists' Magazine*, xvi (1970), 203–11. The surname examples come from R. A McKinley 'The Survey of English Surnames' mentioned above, and his 'The Distribution of Surnames derived from the Names of some Yorkshire towns' in *Tribute to an Antiquary*, 165-175.

For cancer see report in *The Daily Telegraph*, 30 August 1977, 13; for symphalangism see Drs S. G. Elkington and R. G. Huntsman in the *British Medical Journal*, 18 February 1967, 407-11, and F. Leeson, 'The Talbot Fingers', in *Genealogists' Magazine*, xvi (1969), 8–10: for porphyria variegata see *Porphyria – A Royal Malady*, British Medical Association, London, 1968, and a review by Professor A. L. Cochrane in *Genealogists' Magazine*, xvi (1969), 14-15; and for Huntington's Chorea see *Huntington's Chorea*, Association to Combat Huntington's Chorea, London, 1975, and articles in *Sunday Times Colour Supplement*, 28 March 1976, in *Social Work Today*, vi (1976), 787–8, and in *She Magazine*, July, 1975, 72-73.

For the Queen's facial characteristics see O. Forst de

Battaglia, *Traité de Généalogie*, Lausanne, 1949, 98-9. For cousin marriages see B. S. Bramwell, 'Frequency of Cousin Marriages', in *Genealogists' Magazine*, viii (1939), 305-316, and H. C. Pickwick and T. H. Roderick, 'Inbreeding in a Chapman family', in *The American Genealogist*, xxxviii (1962), 240-2.

For intestacy cases see J. A. Cox, *The Recluse of Herald Square: the mystery of Ida E. Wood*, London, 1964; David W. Peck, *The Greer Case: a true court drama*, London, 1963; and Stewart Valdar, *A Brief History of the Jermy family of Norfolk and Suffolk*, London, 1958.

For unclaimed money see *Dormant Funds in Court: Notice to persons requiring information*, Supreme Court Pay Office, pamphlet No. 1293; M. A. Pinhorn, 'Unclaimed Monies', in *Genealogists' Magazine*, xiii (1959), 81-83; and *Unclaimed Money*, by S. H. Preston, London, 1896.

For the Missing Persons Bureau of the Salvation Army see *Genealogists' Magazine*, xviii (1975), 71.

For the claims of the Gardiner family see *The Complete Peerage*, v (1926), 619-20; *Whitaker's Peerage*, 1913; and report in *News Chronicle*, 9 May 1956.

For the Bunyan mementos see R. L. Hine, *Confessions of an Un-common Attorney*, London, 1945, 70. For genealogy and portraits see C. K. Adams, 'Portraiture Problems and Genealogy', in *Genealogists' Magazine*, xiv (1964), 382-8; for the Roffey family see L. R. Muirhead, 'Genealogy – Handmaid of the Arts', in *Genealogists' Magazine*, xii (1956), 224-7.

For the heraldry of Christ Church Gate see P. H. Blake, *Canterbury Cathedral: Christ Church Gate*, Canterbury, 1965; and for the heraldry at Hylton Castle see *The Archaeological Journal*, cxxxiii (1977) 118-34.

For the Mormons and genealogy see *Latter-Day Saint Temples*, The Church of Jesus Christ of Latter-Day Saints, 1958, and *Records Protection in an Uncertain World*, The Genealogical Society, Salt Lake City, n.d., and J. R. Cunningham, 'The Genealogical Work of the Latter-Day Saints', in

Genealogists' Magazine, xiv (1964), 369-73.

For founder's kin see G. D. Squibb, *Founder's Kin: privilege and Pedigree,* Oxford, 1972.

Chapter 10

See in general D. L. Jacobus, *Genealogy as Pastime and Profession,* Baltimore, 1971; *Professional Genealogy Handbook,* Utah Genealogical Association, 1976; and the two leaflets, *Genealogy as a Career,* Society of Genealogists, Leaflet No. 5, 1977, and *Heraldry and Genealogy,* Careers & Occupational Information Centre, Career Outline, 1977.

For the objects of the Society of Genealogists see *The Society of Genealogists of London,* 1911–12, 10–11, and for its collections see A. J. Camp, 'Collections and Indexes of the Society of Genealogists', in *Genealogists' Magazine,* xiii (1961), 311-7.

For the Federation of Family History Societies see their *Federation of Family History Societies: a Handbook,* 1976, and 'Co-operation in Family History Studies' by F. C. Markwell, in *Genealogists' Magazine,* xvii (1974), 618–20.

For one-name studies see F. L. Leeson, 'The Study of Single Surnames and their Distribution', in *Genealogists' Magazine,* xiv (1964), and D. A. Palgrave, 'One-Name Societies', in *Genealogists' Magazine,* xviii (1976), 196-8, and his 'One name activities', in *Family History News and Digest,* i (1977), 55. A *Register of One Name Studies* has now been published.

GENERAL NON-FICTION

0426	Universal/Tandem		
123190	Thomas B. Costain **THE PAGEANT OF ENGLAND:** **1135-1216: THE CONQUERING FAMILY**	£1.50
123271	**1216-1272: THE MAGNIFICENT CENTURY**	£1.50
123352	**1272-1377: THE THREE EDWARDS**	£1.50
123433	**1377-1485: THE LAST PLANTAGENETS**	£1.50
184033	Ben Davidson **THE OFFICIAL FONZIE SCRAPBOOK**	70p* ◆
08571X	Hyam Maccoby **REVOLUTION IN JUDAEA**	75p
168623	Xaviera Hollander **THE HAPPY HOOKER**	80p*
163443	**LETTERS TO THE HAPPY HOOKER**	80p*
168038	**XAVIERA GOES WILD**	80p*
166787	**XAVIERA ON THE BEST PART OF A MAN**	80p*
134265	**XAVIERA!**	80p*
17996X	Xaviera Hollander & Marilyn Chambers **XAVIERA MEETS MARILYN CHAMBERS**	80p*
124901	Fridtjof Nansen **FARTHEST NORTH**	£1.00
175158	Sakuzawa Nyoiti **MACROBIOTICS**	50p*
181638	Suze Randall **SUZE**	75p*
180755	Grant Tracy Saxon **THE HAPPY HUSTLER**	70p
134931	La Leche League **THE WOMANLY ART OF BREASTFEEDING**	60p
141970	Erna Wright **THE NEW CHILDBIRTH**	75p
067282	**THE NEW CHILDHOOD**	75p
054938	**PERIODS WITHOUT PAIN**	60p
0426	Hanau Distribution	
087232	David Lewis **SEXPIONAGE**	70p
087151	**THE SECRET LIFE OF ADOLPH HITLER**	75p
086864	Linda Lovelace **INSIDE LINDA LOVELACE**	60p
086945	**THE INTIMATE DIARY OF LINDA LOVELACE**	60p
086007	Gerard I. Nierenberg & Henry H. Calero **HOW TO READ A PERSON LIKE A BOOK**	95p

† For sale in Britain and Ireland only.
*Not for sale in Canada.
◆ Film & T.V. tie-ins.

GENERAL NON-FICTION

0352	Star	
301392	Linda Blandford **OIL SHEIKHS**	95p
396121	Anthony Cave Brown **BODYGUARD OF LIES (Large Format)**	£1.95*
301368	John Dean **BLIND AMBITION**	£1.00*
300124	Dr. F. Dodson **HOW TO PARENT**	75p*
301457	**THE FAMILY DICTIONARY OF SYMPTOMS**	95p*
398914	J. Paul Getty **HOW TO BE RICH**	60p*
397829	**HOW TO BE A SUCCESSFUL EXECUTIVE**	60p*
398566	Harry Lorayne & Jerry Lucas **THE MEMORY BOOK**	60p*
39692X	Henry Miller **THE WORLD OF SEX**	60p
395311	Neville Randall & Gary Keane **FOCUS ON FACT:** **THE WORLD OF INVENTION (illus)**	75p
39532X	**THE STORY OF SPORT (illus)**	75p
39529X	**THE PSYCHIC WORLD (illus)**	75p
395303	**THE STORY OF CHRISTMAS (illus)**	75p
395338	**UNSOLVED MYSTERIES (illus)**	75p
397640	David Reuben **HOW TO GET MORE OUT OF SEX**	85p*
398779	Fiona Richmond **FIONA**	50p
396040	Idries Shah **THE SUFIS (Large Format)**	£1.95
395478	Michael Smith **THE DUCHESS OF DUKE STREET ENTERTAINS**	£1.50◆

†For sale in Britain and Ireland only.
*Not for sale in Canada.
◆ Film & T.V. tie-ins.

Wyndham Books are obtainable from many booksellers and newsagents. If you have any difficulty please send purchase price plus postage on the scale below to:

Wyndham Cash Sales:
P O Box 11,
Falmouth,
Cornwall.

or

Star Book Service:
G P O Box 29,
Douglas,
Isle of Man,
British Isles.

While every effort is made to keep prices low, it is sometimes necessary to increase prices at short notice. Wyndham Books reserve the right to show new retail prices on covers which may differ from those advertised in the text or elsewhere.

Postage and Packing Rate

UK

22p for the first book plus 10p per copy for each additional book ordered to a maximum charge of 82p.

BFPO and Eire

22p for the first book, plus 10p per copy for the next 6 books and thereafter 4p per book.

Overseas

30p for the first book and 10p per copy for each additional book.

These charges are subject to Post Office charge fluctuations.